Go Play!

The Importance of Unstructured Play in Our Digital Age

BOB HERMES

The information in this book is designed to impart information to help individuals in making positive changes in their lives. The ideas presented are not meant to substitute for medical care or psychological assistance.

Published by:

Artichoke Press, LLC.
Missoula, MT
(406) 549-9813

ISBN-13:978-1726411295

ISBN-10:172641129X

CONTENTS

Foreword   i

Introduction   5

1   Play: A Short History   9

2   Digital Changes It All   21

3   More Than Duck, Duck, Goose: 39
     The Serious Business of Play

4   Receding Recess   51

5   Helicopter Parents and Head Games: 61
     A Lesson in Forced Play

6   Playing It Safe   73

7   Play for Adults   81

Conclusion   87

Easy, Engaging Games for 3 or More Players 91

About the Author   115

Afterword   119

FOREWORD

Michael was born on May 17, 1957
and passed away on Saturday, August 18, 2018.

"Hey, guys, looks like the Landes are home. Wanna see if they're up for a game of street football? Looks like we have enough now for four-on-four. The Millhouses' streetlight will be the goal line for one end zone, and the corner streetlight will be the goal line for the other end zone. Rushers must count one-thousand-one, one-thousand-two, and it's one hand touch below the waste."

Everyone agrees and we are off to play another neighborhood game of football.

Bob Hermes and I have known each other since we were eleven years old. We were part of a neighborhood gang who were outside playing most of the day, and a majority of the summer nights.

Our friendship continued into high school, when we became teammates in football and wrestling. In the years since high school we've worked together in a number of youth sports programs in our community.

While these programs have been invaluable, it is my belief that as a society we have become *over-organized* and are forcing our kids to become specialized at a very early age. You will read about some of this in this book.

I remember well a challenge Bob gave me at the end of our freshman season of wrestling: eat six hamburgers and one pound of French fries. It was a gentleman's bet and I couldn't pass it up. I also truly believed I could do it. So off to his parents' business, Hermes Hamburgers, we went.

Now, we had just finished our wrestling season. Wrestlers in that day and age usually cut weight and didn't eat a lot of food during the season.

I got five of the six burgers down, along with the pound of fries, but I certainly didn't feel too well after. It was a small price to pay, though, for the true friendship forged that day.

As you read the following pages, I think you will be amazed at how our society has set aside our ability to just play, and with it, unique opportunities to learn the basic skills we need to get along or settle differences with others. This is due in large part to the evolution of the computer and how technology has changed the way so many people handle their daily lives.

Since the first humans walked the Earth, we've used our God-given imagination for a great many things, including play. Today's games, however, have taken the need for that imagination away from the individual and replaced it with computers.

Now, there is nothing wrong with utilizing technology; in many ways it has served society well. That said, it is my personal belief that we have allowed, even encouraged, our kids to start using technology at too young an age. This means that we have not taught them to use their imagination to make up and play games on their own or as part of a group.

People today also face more health challenges than ever before. Again, evidence points to technological changes and the resulting lack of physical and imaginative mental exercise.

One of our biggest challenges, though, is keeping families together so parents have time to spend with their kids and hopefully show them some of the outdoor games they played as children. It will take all of us in the village to help work on this one!

I feel blessed to have grown up in a time when the world moved at a much slower and more peaceful pace, where kids were out playing whatever game they decided to play and learning the skills to manage any differences or disputes on their own. I am also humbled and honored to have been asked to write this foreword for my friend Bob.

It is my sincerest wish that as you read this book, you will recall the adventures of your own childhood and recognize that what our kids – and our society – need most is the freedom to play and the opportunity to use the imagination God has given us.

Mike McChesney

INTRODUCTION

Play is an instinctive activity that can be seen in various forms in every society across the globe. It has numerous physical, mental and emotional benefits, in both the short- and long-term.

Through play, we learn new skills and continually improve upon them, thus giving us confidence. Play also teaches us to both collaborate and compete with others, to work out our differences through "sportsmanship" rather than aggression, and to win or lose with grace.

This is true, relatively speaking, not only for humans, but in the animal world as well. Young monkeys, lions, and bear cubs all use play to prepare them for hunting and socializing in the real world. Have you ever taken your kids or grandkids to the zoo and watched the monkeys teasing each other? They enjoy playing "chase" or "take-away" as much as the kids. Just as important, play is a source of joy and balance in life.

We have all heard the saying, "All work and no play makes John a dull boy." One need only look at today's world—high in stress and often low in tolerance or patience to see the truth of it. John is not only dull, but also anxious, depressed and feeling isolated in life.

This book explores the many ways in which play aids in mental, physical and spiritual development, and facilitates continued growth and joy throughout our lives. It will also discuss the changes around child's play that have occurred over the past several decades. These changes will be discussed with regard to the potentially harmful shift from "free" play to overregulated activities and the reliance on videogames and digital technology.

These days, we have plenty of "toys" but very little "play." True play is best experienced when it is free, spontaneous, joyful and done in parks, playgrounds and open areas that allow for carefree activities.

Organic, unfettered play teaches children to appreciate and follow rules. It also helps them develop their problem-solving skills as they move from concrete to abstract thought. Finally, play is an excellent way for children to build social skills and confidence.

It is through play that friendships are built. Friendships are the basis for all other relationships in life. Marriage, jobs, neighbors and parenting need a foundation of friendship and respect for others to succeed.

Unfortunately, natural, spontaneous play has vastly decreased over the past several years. This generation has been called "Gen D," a.k.a., ADD generation. According to LS:N Global, "They can't imagine a world without computers, mobile phones and the Internet.

They skitter, haul, mod and hack. Natural born multitaskers, they pack 11 hours of online entertainment into 7.5 hours. This is the first native digital generation. This is Generation D."[1]

Usually when you think of ADD, your mind goes to Attention Deficit Disorder. But this nickname refers to how consumer-driven media fosters ADD types of behaviors. One example is "frazzing," a word for the frenzied multi-tasking of jumping from one device to another. This overwhelms the brain and short-circuits concentration.

Whereas kids used to spend the daylight hours riding their bikes and playing tag, they now sit hunched over computers, their hands clenching a mouse or controller.

---

[1] LS:N Global. (2010, April 10). Generation D. Retrieved August 11, 2018, from https://www.lsnglobal.com/macro-trends/article/2685/generation-d

Go Play! seeks to remind parents, teachers, and other caregivers of the many benefits of natural play and the steps they can take introduce (or reintroduce) it into their kids' lives.

Hopefully, it will also encourage adults to evaluate their own schedules – however busy they may be – and incorporate time for play whenever possible. You don't have to be a kid to exhibit ADD tendencies. We could all use a break from screen time, especially to help us focus on the things that really matter.

CHAPTER 1

PLAY: A SHORT HISTORY

Play has been a part of human development since the beginning of early man. The ancient Egyptians danced, played field hockey, swam and wrestled. They also played with dolls and board games.[2] In Persia, children as young as six played with slings, bows and javelins; they also went horseback riding.

The Greeks in particular were committed to physical fitness – every city had a public gymnasium – and play was considered an integral part of maintaining a healthy mind, body and spirit.

Organized activities like wrestling, track and field events and gymnastics aided in the development of their youth and sporting events were well attended.[3]

---

[2] Mark, Joshua J. "Games, Sports & Recreation in Ancient Egypt." *Ancient History Encyclopedia.* Last modified April 11, 2017. https://www.ancient.eu/article/1036/.

[3] Carr, K.E. What games did people play in ancient Greece?. Quatr.us Study Guides, July 6, 2017. Web. May 1, 2018.

In Sparta, children as young as seven threw javelins, swam, wrestled, hiked and ran. Athenian children engaged in free play that included games with balls and hoops – precursors to modern basketball; they also swung and played Blind Man's Bluff (a form of tag),[4] hide-and-seek and, from a young age, learned boxing and gymnastics.

Palaestras were areas specifically developed and set aside as wrestling grounds. Discus throwing, or the tossing of a heavy disc to see who could get it the farthest, was memorialized in the fifth century by famed Athenian sculptor Myron in his statue, the Discobolus.[5]

In 776 BC, the Greeks created the first Olympic games as part of a religious ceremony in honor of Zeus.

The training for these games was essentially a more intense version of play; it fostered a spirit of competition and achieving one's personal best while adhering to rules of respect and sportsmanship.

In the seventh century, they added horse racing and chariot racing.

Discus throwing was lost for a while, and then

---

[4] Wikipedia contributors, "Blind man's buff," *Wikipedia, The Free Encyclopedia*, https://en.wikipedia.org/w/index.php?title=Blind_man%27s_buff&oldid=819551082 (accessed May 1, 2018).

[5] "Discus throwing." The Columbia Encyclopedia, 6th ed. *Encyclopedia.com*. (May 1, 2018). http://www.encyclopedia.com/reference/encyclopedias-almanacs-transcripts-and-maps/discus-throwing

rediscovered in Germany in the 1870s. Though the techniques have varied over time, it has been part of the modern Summer Olympic Games since they began in 1896.

As we shifted into modern times, the world changed exponentially, yet the concept of play remained largely unchanged. My own mother was raised on a farm in North Dakota during the 1930s. She enjoyed recounting stories of her favorite childhood games and play activities.

She did not have the latest fancy toys – and there were certainly no digital games back then. She, along with her five siblings and their friends, had to use whatever they had available in their environment.

They had to create their own fun – and their own adventures – every day. Sometimes they played a board game in the farmhouse basement, but the majority of their time was spent outside. They had fun playing games like Red-light, Green-light that lasted for hours.

The players would mark a starting line and a finish line, then one child would be chosen as "traffic cop." The others would stand on the starting line, then race forward when the cop called out "Green Light!"

When cop called "Red Light!" they had to freeze in their tracks. The first person to reach the finish line was the winner.

This simple game kept them physically fit and taught them

to follow rules, but all they knew that it was fun!

Mom's favorite game took place in the winter. After a heavy snowfall, her father would pull out a couple of scoop shovels from the barn, and she and her sisters and brothers would run to the nearby coal hills. There, they would sit in the scoop part of the shovel, hold onto the handle, and race their makeshift sleds down the hill.

Over and over, they would walk back up, all the while anticipating those moments of carefree abandon when they would fly down and see who the fastest sibling was.

Hearing Mom tell the stories, I could almost hear the squeals of pure joy. As enthralled kids, we could see their spent but exuberant faces as they returned to the house for a hot, home-cooked meal.

My mom got such joy just from telling the stories and laughing about the antics of the kids that she would have all of us kids laughing along with her.

The same was true when my brother Dean and I were children. Playing with others was seen as an essential, natural part of life. My friends, siblings and I had sports for every season. My childhood friend Mike McChesney shared some of those stories in the foreword to this book.

We played mostly with our neighbors; sometimes our parents even joined in after work. We'd appear in the parks with ball glove and bat or football in hand, prepared to play.

We played outside well past sundown or until our mothers called us in for supper, homework or bed.

While playing, we'd solve our own disputes and strengthen our friendships, without intervention from adults. We were living out what are now being called "free range childhoods." This is the concept of raising children in the spirit of encouraging them to function independently and with limited adult supervision.

Free Range Parents are the opposite of "Helicopter Parents" who hover over all of the activities of their child. They are always ready to step in and solve problems, without allowing the kids to learn from their own mistakes.

Dean and I have many fond memories of growing up on those North Dakota plains. All summer long we'd leave the house after breakfast and embark on a new adventure with our cousins and neighborhood friends.

"Be home for lunch," our mother would say as she shooed us out. After lunch, she'd tell us only to be home by dark. Other than those hastily eaten meals, we ran, jumped and explored from sunup to sundown.

"We never had such a thing as an organized sport," Dean recalls. "Everything we did came from our own inventions. We didn't need Chuck E. Cheese or Gymboree – the world was our playground.

We roamed the neighborhood, playing in neighbor's yards,

gardens and with their farm machinery, and our long list of imaginary friends included everyone from Roy Rogers and Gene Autry to General Custer and the Sioux hordes."

Dean also remembers one neighbor that had a wrecked airboat in his backyard alley. We imagined and used it as everything from a stagecoach under attack from the Indians, to a riverboat trying to outrun the ship of pirates gaining on us.

One of Dean's favorite places was our cousins' farm on the edge of town, about a quarter-mile from our house. It was a marvelous place to explore and there let our imaginations run wild. Our best find was the foundation of an old shed that had been torn down.

We hauled branches and other tree limbs from creeks and coulees far and wide to make a roof over the depression left by the shed. After we had fashioned our hideout, we went into the hills around town and collected stones called mica, which we hauled to the fort by the pailful. This was our "gold," which we sized, stacked and prized as much as any treasure.

The arrival of winter brought sledding on the town hill, snowball fights, and huge snow forts that served as our base of operations for hours-long snowball fights with our rivals. Our only organized play came on Sunday afternoon: the church hall was turned into a roller-skating rink.

After the church services, our parents would give us each a nickel – the cost of a skate rental – so we would get out of their hair for a few hours. "Don't come home until four," we were told, and we were only happy to comply.

My brother's introduction to organized sports came his freshman year of high school, when he joined the football and wrestling teams. He eagerly threw himself into both sports, and with plenty of hard work, found he excelled at them.

Dean remembers, "It was the first time I ever played football, and I knew absolutely nothing. I must have learned fast, though, because by the time I was a senior I was an All-State tackle and my team was in the championships."

He loved wrestling as well. Uniforms were a pair of dyed long johns with school-colored shorts; there were no tops. They practiced on four-by-eight throw mats covered with a canvas. As a senior, he was a State Champion.

Both sports made a lasting impression on Dean, and after graduating from college he returned to his high school as the football and wrestling coach, as well as a teacher. Over the next thirty-five years he would touch the lives of thousands of students; he also had ample opportunity to observe the changing attitudes around sports and play in general.

Dean had this to say about his experiences: "When I started coaching in 1967, my school only allowed junior high intramurals; there was no travel for any team except Varsity. It was a great policy because it gave those younger kids a chance to learn about our offense and defense rather than focusing on playing opponents. When they got to the Varsity they understood our program.

"This slowly changed over the years into a competitive program at every grade, from junior high to Varsity. I never liked the change, but parents got more and more involved and demanded competition.

In my thirty-five years, I saw many changes in kids. They certainly stimulate their imaginations differently than we did, but they still have imaginations and they still play.

"In my 35 years of coaching sports and teaching, I witnessed many changes in participation forms. During my first years of working, only intramural competition was allowed starting in the 7th grade. No out-of-town competition was allowed.

As the head coach I had my sub-Varsity coaches teach the kids in all the elementary schools the offense and defensive schemes the Varsity teams used.

"We limited the offense to six running plays and two pass plays. The defense was limited to basic 5-2 defense with no stunts. When the kids got to the Varsity level as sophomores in high school, they were very skilled in the basics. Only then did we teach them plays and defensive stunts. Kids became very proficient and really knew their plays. The things they learned cut down on mistakes and made our teams much better.

"The winning that resulted drew more and more kids to come out and our teams were always very competitive. As a result, the kids loved sports and wanted to be a team member.

"In the middle of my career, more and more parents demanded kids be allowed to participate at younger ages and that the kids be allowed to compete in out-of-town games. Soon we had teams all the way down to the 3rd grade with parents coaching and using their own offenses and defenses.

"Consequently, by the time they reached our Varsity as sophomores they were less skilled, and we had to spend more and more time teaching them the basics. Mistakes increased, and performance suffered. Wins were hard to achieve, and interest and turnout suffered.

"This happened in all sports – from football to track. Kids who had, in earlier years, participated in many sports now specialized. They became less and less interested in teamwork and helping each other achieve. Instead, they became much more self-absorbed and never developed the close relationships necessary for team success. Now we get some great individual performances, but seldom win a team championship."

Though I followed a different career path than my brother, I knew exactly what he was talking about. There were drastic differences between the way my generation played and the way my own sons did.

They didn't go outside nearly as much, and play was less a group activity and more often involved only a child or two, joysticks, and the screen of the latest video game.

The digital age, with all its conveniences, was upon us. Though I would caution myself not to assume the new ways were all bad and things were perfect back in the "good old days," I couldn't help but wonder what my boys were missing out on.

Although decades had passed, I could still vividly recall the games I had played as a kid, and everyone I had played with. I highly doubted my kids would remember a particular Xbox or PlayStation game a year later, let alone twenty or thirty years after the fact.

I began to really think about free play, and its importance, not just for recreation, but also in every aspect of our lives. Were we, I wondered, doing today's children a disservice by limiting (or eliminating) free play in favor of technology's latest toys?

Since then, the use of technology in all areas of life has increased exponentially, encompassing not only play and recreation, but nearly every human interaction.

I began speaking to people my age and older – some even in their eighties – who remembered like it was yesterday the games they played on their families' farms back in the 1930s and 40s. Tag, Hide and Go Seek, or baseball – even just remembering the made-up games made them smile. Whatever their game of choice, it contributed to their creativity and innovative spirits; it helped form who they would become as adults.

I also interviewed university professors, high school teachers and coaches who, like my brother, have witnessed the development of thousands of students. They all spoke of the marked differences in use of imagination as well as playing games with friends and family over the past twenty or so years.

When our kids play games they have the opportunity to sharpen many skills. They can learn logic, reasoning, strategy, and especially social skills. They could be plotting their next move in chess, or taking turns in Foursquare. Games are a great way to gain confidence

My conclusion? That it is of vital importance for families and communities to bring back some of the lessons of natural play and all it entails: children interacting face-to-face and expressing genuine emotions, rather than online or over text messages.

As a society and community, we need to offer

opportunities to our children and our children's children to run, play, explore, build forts out of old trees or cardboard. In other words, we need to teach them to play.

Here is a fun way to choose up sides, settle an argument or play a quick round of easy outs.

Rock/Paper/Scissors

This is an old "choosing game" turned into a cooperative running game.

The sign for a rock is a fist. The sign for paper is a fully open hand. The scissors sign is a hand with the fingers pointing outward.

The order is: Rock smashes scissors; scissors cut paper; paper covers rock. Each sign can therefore beat one other sign, and each sign is vulnerable to one other sign.

There are two teams. The playing area is divided into a safety zone at each end and has a centerline in the middle.

The teams huddle behind the center line and decide which sign they are going to use. Then each team approaches the center line, and at a count of three, everyone calls out, "Rock, paper, scissors" and uses the sign that was decide upon. Whichever team wins chases the other back to their safety areas. Any player tagged before he or she reaches the safety zone changes sides.

Now regroup with your new lineup and start the game over. If both teams use the same sign, everyone must go back and choose a sign again.

CHAPTER 2

DIGITAL CHANGES IT ALL

By the early 1980s, the world looked vastly different from when I was a kid: we were in a nuclear arms race with the Soviet Union; Sally Ride became the first woman in space; and everyone wanted to know, "Who Shot JR?"

In 1980, Pac-Man and the Rubik's Cube also made their debut, yet unstructured play on the whole remained largely unchanged. Most children still spent much of their time outside, whether that meant throwing a Frisbee around their backyards, or, in the cities, playing stickball in the streets.

Video games were a novelty and housed mostly in arcades. If you were lucky enough to have one in your town, your parents might give you a few dollars to play Space Invaders or Centipede. These were special occasions – perhaps a treat for good behavior or a birthday – they did not replace organic free play.

The same was true when the first home consoles for video

games came out. Every kid wanted an Atari for Christmas, but again, it was seen as a supplement to other activities. Staying inside on a sunny summer day with only a TV and a joystick for company was considered a waste of time, and unhealthy to boot.

Aside from school, play was still the primary vehicle for physical and mental fitness. Repetitive movement such as swinging a baseball bat all afternoon or twisting and turning to avoid being tagged "it" improved one's eye-hand coordination and motor skills.

Teachers, parents and coaches encouraged active play as a way to prevent obesity and promote overall health. And those were just the physical benefits!

In using whatever tools were at their disposal – be it those scoop shovels my mother used to slide down the snowy hills or twigs and branches my brother used to make a fort – kids tapped into their own inventiveness and creativity, which in turn helped build their confidence.

They also learned to assess a situation and use critical thinking to make decisions; how to compete and collaborate; the need for diplomacy, debate and advocacy; and how to cultivate relationships and navigate society.

In short, they used these skills needed to become well-adjusted, successful and productive adults. They learned the most valuable skill needed in any workplace: problem solving.

Video games started out like any other toy. They rose to popularity and faded just as quickly; in fact, many considered them a fad. Behind the scenes, however, a true technological revolution was taking place, and no one – at least not the average person – could have anticipated the radical ways in which it would soon change our world.

That said, the path of the home gaming industry has been anything but smooth; in fact, it almost went to the graveyard of history before it really got started.

Most of us have heard of the dot-com boom (and bust) that occurred between 1997 and 2001 – a period of unprecedented growth and wild market speculation around the Internet, including the creation of countless Internet-based startups.

Many of these companies later went belly-up when the bubble burst. Far fewer people recall the implosion of the North American gaming industry of 1983; however, its shockwaves were felt throughout the technological world.

By 1981, video arcades were a five-billion-dollar-a-year industry; and, after a slow start in the 1970s, the home console gaming industry had also taken off. Atari was leading the pack, with many experts citing its 1980 release of Space Invaders (for the Atari 2600) as the pivotal moment.

Begun as a two-man operation in California in 1972, by the late '70s Atari had become the kingpin of the electronics industry, producing home computers, home gaming consoles and arcade games. It also created some of the earliest gaming hits such as Pong, Pitfall and Frogger.

Atari held its own in the home computer market against such competitors as the Commodore 64 and IBM, only to be threatened from within.

In 1979, a group of game designers, disgruntled because of Atari's refusal to give them credit or pay them royalties, left to form their own company. This venture, Activision, became the first third-party developer.

Atari immediately sued for trademark infringement, but the court refused to grant them a restraining order. Eventually Atari settled the case, essentially giving the green light to every other company from Quaker Oats to Purina to jump on the bandwagon.

Suddenly, stores were flooded with inexpensive, low-quality games.

This oversaturation was credited with causing the "video game crash of 1983," a massive implosion of the North American market. That year, Atari itself reported a whopping $535-million dollar loss.[6]

Ironically, it was Japan, the U.S.'s largest business

---

[6] Wikipedia contributors. "Video game crash of 1983," *Wikipedia, The Free Encyclopedia,* https://en.wikipedia.org/w/index.php?title=Video_game_crash_of_1983&oldid=835944266 (accessed May 1, 2018).

competitor, which brought about the resurgence of the gaming system in America. Japan had always been a major player in the gaming business.

Founded in 1955, the Tokyo-based company Namco was originally an operator of children's games in department stores. Within two decades it found itself presented with a unique opportunity to position itself within the nascent video game industry.

By the mid-70s, Atari's Japanese subsidiary was struggling. In a move that many thought misguided, Namco outbid competitors to buy Atari Japan for $500,000; the purchase, however, included exclusive distribution rights of Atari games in Japan for the next ten years.

Namco would also leave another indelible mark on the gaming industry, in Japan and around the world. In 1977 a twenty-something named Toru Iwantani joined the company.

Iwantani had no formal training in computers or graphics; however, since childhood he had liked to scribble *manga*, or Japanese cartoons, in his schoolbooks.

He would later credit these manga as the inspiration for his video game creation, among them a simple yet thoroughly addictive game called "Pakku-Man."

Namco released the game in Japan in May of 1977, to rave reviews. Three years later, Pac-Man would become an immediate and permanent fixture among American game lovers of all ages.[7]

By 1985, the home console business in the U.S. was all but nonexistent, with investors and entertainment experts alike writing it off as a fad. This was not the case in other countries, however, and that's when another Japanese gaming company, Nintendo, decided to step in.

Despite the skepticism of the gaming press, the company unveiled its Nintendo Gaming System at the 1985 Consumer Electronics Show; one year later it was launched to the American public.[8]

Nintendo had been careful to avoid its predecessors' mistakes; third-party developers had to adhere to strict regulations. A "lock-and-key" system was also used to thwart reverse engineering.

Over the next decade, Nintendo would go on to sell sixty million units before being discontinued in the U.S. One of its original games – Super Mario Bros. – remains one of the bestselling games of all time.

Most importantly, Nintendo revitalized the gaming market

[7] Jones, Tegan, "The History of Pac-Man," Today I Found Out, http://www.todayifoundout.com/index.php/2013/08/the-history-of-pac-man/ (accessed May 1, 2018).

[8] Rossen, Jake, "How Nintendo Conquered Manhattan in 1985," Mental Floss, http://mentalfloss.com/article/62232/how-nintendo-conquered-manhattan-1985 (accessed May 1, 2018).

in America and inspired future generations of game creators and players alike.

Fast-forward to the late '90s and early 2000s, and the rise of the "first-person shooter." As the name suggests, this video game genre allows the player to operate from the first-person perspective of the main character, usually a hero, who must take down the enemy.

Originally conceived in the 1970s, first-person shooter games did not become commercially popular until the mid-to-late 1990s. This happened with the release of games like "Golden Eye 007," based on the James Bond movie, and "Tom Clancy's Rainbow Six," which, like Clancy's novels, had a counterterrorism theme.

These games were instant and enormous successes; in fact, as of 2004, "Golden Eye 007" was still Nintendo 64's bestselling game. In the years that followed, advancements in 3-D graphics, multilevel narratives and widespread multiplayer platforms made these games increasingly immersive.

Players could run, jump and climb through any terrain – from the seaside to the desert – all from the comfort of their couch. They also, inevitably, had weapons and a singular goal: to destroy the enemy.

For children, the goal became less about interacting with

real-life peers and more about besting a computer program.[9] Parents and educators began worrying about what the effects of the violence on television and video games might have on their children.

In and of itself, the evolution of gaming might not have been so impactful or even noteworthy to the general public. However, as part of the overarching technological changes sweeping the globe, it has contributed to the remaking (and some say demise) of the childhood experience.

Since the late 1990s, widespread Internet use has made our world more connected in a digital sense, but it has also resulted in much more physical isolation.

These factors, coupled with other changes – such as the need for two-income households and parents becoming more concerned about their children in an unsafe world – drastically decreased the amount of time kids spent in free play.

Kids started spending more and more time in front of a computer and less and less time playing tag in the yard. Called "latch-key kids," they were instructed to stay inside and allow no one in the house until one or more of the parents came home.

---

[9] Jenson, K. Thor, "The Complete History of First Person Shooters," Geek Squad, https://www.geek.com/games/the-complete-history-of-first-person-shooters-1713135/ (accessed May 1, 2018)

This also greatly affected socialization. Children played games against themselves or with online opponents, which meant a decrease in in-person interaction.

I personally would not go as far as to say there is no connection between players, because I have heard tell of a young boy who brags about writing Japanese and reading Japanese, but cannot speak the language. This is because he is playing against a video game opponent in Japan.

This sort of connection is certainly less impactful and requires less accountability than a game of softball. When there is a disagreement, one need not deal with the other person; they can just sign off the game and make them disappear. There is no way to learn conflict management or how to read body language in a disagreement.

Over the years, technology has continued to move at breakneck speed, completely transforming the way we work, learn and communicate. Back in the day, we had regular face-to-face interactions with our friends, family and colleagues, and perhaps a pen pal here or there.

Now, it is largely the opposite, with people regularly "speaking" via email, texts and social media, oftentimes never meeting in person or even over the phone. As impactful as this has been for adults, it is exponentially more so for children, some of whom may never know what it is like to communicate organically.

All of these changes have created a completely different social landscape. Today's children expect instant communication, instant gratification and instant entertainment.

While the ramifications of this will not be fully realized for some time, I – along with a number of others – suspect that many of the ways in which children spend their time is extremely detrimental to their mental, emotional and physical health – not to mention society as a whole.

Kids get little to no physical exercise, leading to unprecedented levels of childhood obesity. According to the American Heart Association, one in three children and teens in the U.S. are overweight or obese.

Furthermore, childhood obesity has tripled from 1971 to 2011.[10] While there are several factors associated with this – including increased portion sizes – the statistics track the decline in activity resulting from a lack of the free play activities described earlier.

There is also a vast difference in the intellectual stimulation kids get from video games. These games present few challenges and little opportunity to develop problem-solving skills.

---

[10] American Heart Association, "Overweight in Children," http://www.heart.org/HEARTORG/HealthyLiving/HealthyKids/ChildhoodObesity/Overweight-in-Children_UCM_304054_Article.jsp#.Wupzle8vyW8 (Accessed May 1, 2018)

Current games have interactive components that allow gamers to play against strangers, whom they know only by their gamer names, often in different countries and with different moral values.

Hours and hours are dedicated to online contests, and many games glorify violence and destroying the other gamers – no diplomacy or cooperation needed. Most disturbing, some companies have also added vulgar, pornographic images and sexual encounters to certain games.

These games not only forfeit real relationships in favor of make-believe interactions with digital images; they also impact kids' abilities to form relationships offline.

Some children suffer from addiction to video games and even need medical treatment for the various physical and mental disorders that develop as a result. The World Health Organization recently decided to add "gaming disorder" to its official list of mental health conditions, stating that gaming behavior could qualify as problematic if it interferes significantly in other areas of peoples' lives.

I personally know one family who dealt with such a crisis. One of their four children spent most of his time gaming in his parents' basement. He played various games, including Xbox "Madden Football" and a cops and robbers game.

He would play after school, through dinner, and late into the night. Eventually the gaming took away his ability for restful sleep, which led to narcolepsy. He also developed severe depression, withdrew from family and friends, and dropped out of school due to his inability to focus. This former honor roll student and outstanding athlete wound up trapped in a dark place of seclusion and isolation.

Sick with worry, his parents searched throughout the country for doctors and specialists who could help their family. After years of suffering, he has seen some relief, but he still has trouble fully concentrating.

Of course, not everyone experiences such an extreme reaction to gaming as my friend's son. However, the potential for this situation does exist. I am not condemning all technology, nor am I suggesting that parents can halt the march of "progress" or completely stop their children from texting or using social media.

For better or worse, electronic devices have become an integral part of the fabric of our society. Nevertheless, I am advocating for parents to recognize the enormity of the influence technology has on their children.

I encourage all of us to make an informed attempt to balance it with a return to the benefits of old-fashioned free play.

The following chapters will discuss how parents can do this in safe, productive ways that engender *organic* connectedness and creativity.

First, though, it is important to provide ways in which they can stop videogames from becoming a problem. Here are some tips, followed by a much beloved free-play game from my own childhood.

Tips for Parents and Caregivers

For today's parents and often caregivers, battling technology can feel like an uphill battle. Everywhere we look, computers, smartphones, smart TVs, iPads, and gaming consoles surround us.

It appears that every minute our children are being texted, video-messaged, or targeted by social media and gaming companies.

However, there are still several common sense measures parents can take to help their children enjoy video games and interactive shows in a healthy way. Actually, these strategies are not all that different from monitoring what movies your child goes to see or what television shows they watch.

Just like you would prevent your preschooler from watching violent or sexually explicit movies, it would be a good idea to keep them away from video games altogether. Even the most benign games are most likely inappropriate for such young children.

The earlier they start playing video games, the more likely it is that they will become addicted.

If and when you do decide to let your child play, make sure you check the Electronic Software Ratings Board (ESRB) ratings of each game he or she is interested in, with regard to both the content and level of development. It is not enough to put the filters on their phone or video device. You must also put it on your television.

All store-bought video games are evaluated by the ESRB and rated for their appropriateness for children and teens. The ratings are featured prominently on the game packaging.

Studies of children exposed to violent media have shown that they may become numb to violence in real life or possibly even imitate the violence. Younger children and those with emotional, behavioral or learning problems may be more susceptible to violent images.

Some early education thought leaders have called the phone or iPad the "Third Parent" or "Instant Baby-Sitter." Most of us have been out to dinner and seen a parent slide the baby in the high chair and hand them their cell phone so the child will be entertained and the adults can visit.

Once appropriate games have been chosen, make the time to play with your children. This will allow you to see the content for yourself and discuss it with them. It is also an excellent opportunity to enjoy a shared experience.

Even if you approve of the game, you should set clear rules about game content in general. There must be some agreement about playing time and location (e.g., kids must play in the living room or study, as opposed to their bedroom where it would be unsupervised, and playing can happen only after homework and/or chores are done). These rules should apply whether they are home or elsewhere (such as a friend's house).

You should also remain vigilant about monitoring your child's online interactions and warning them about potential dangers while playing games online. Be especially aware if your child shows distress, as they could be victims of "cyber-bullying" online in chat rooms or on Facebook.

Be sure to encourage your child's participation in other activities, particularly physical activities. And remember, you are your child's role model in all areas, including their video game and online activity. "Do as I say, not as I do," is not excellent parenting advice. For the most part, your children will follow your lead, whether they realize it or not.

If you want them to spend less time on their screens, put your phone down and engage with them.

If, despite taking these precautions, you have concerns about your child's gaming habits, or if your child is having difficulty with his/her moods or behavior, ask your pediatrician, family physician, or school counselor to help arrange a referral to a trained and qualified mental health professional.

Another tip here would be to make sure there is free time away from digital devices everyday and allocate one hour or more of free play outside at a park or schoolyard-type setting where physical activity can occur.

Play catch, run, jog, or walk together and take time to visit while connecting with each other about what is happening in each other's lives. This sounds simple, but it is critical to emotional well-being and will develop a closeness that will protect your child like a force field around them.

While coaching youth wrestling, I would offer the kids trivia moments prior to the start of practice. I would arrive fifteen minutes early to practice and ask whoever arrived early questions about wrestling and school history, and offer ice cream awards for a certain number of correct answers.

Not only did this encourage participants to get to practice on time, it had a mesmerizing effect on them. They would pay attention and not goof off before the start of practice.

I would have athletes asking for more trivia questions each week of the years we ran our wrestling program. The program grew in popularity every year, and I know this simple trivia challenge helped keep us organized throughout the season.

It also built a connection with the team and the adult leaders who were there to mentor and guide them.

Any encouragement adults give to help kids to be active and involved is time well spent.

The next game involves a hoop and a ball and a willingness to have fun.

How to Play "21"

This game allows players to engage in a lighthearted competition while improving their basketball skills. One of the best things about "21" is that there is no set number of players — no time is wasted waiting for more people to show up, and no one ever has to stand around waiting for their chance to play.

Each player gets a turn shooting three shots at the basket, with the first shot, taken from the free-throw line, being worth three points. The second shot is worth two points and taken from the location the player rebounded the first shot from.

He or she therefore tries to get the rebound close to the basket and hustles to get to that spot quickly. The third shot is worth one point and can be taken from anywhere on the court. If the player makes all three shots, they get to go again for another three shots.

The first player to reach 21 points is the winner. Best of all, the game is gender-neutral and players of all ages may compete. We often had everyone from young children to parents and grandparents participating, making it an excellent opportunity for bonding.

Does your child catch a school bus? Perhaps you can invest in a basketball hoop and encourage the students to play "21" while they wait for the bus.

CHAPTER 3

MORE THAN DUCK, DUCK, GOOSE:
THE SERIOUS BUSINESS OF PLAY

Adults often view children at play with a combination of wistful longing and good-natured patronizing. They dismiss kids' behavior as "cute" and reminisce about the days when they too engaged in similar "wastes of time." They feel nostalgia for a time before they had to get down to the serious business of living.

The truth is more complex: play is an integral function of a child's development.[11] This is just not speculation or a theory bandied about on Twitter or Facebook, but a fact

---

[11] Ginsburg, Kenneth R. and the Committee on Communications, and the Committee on Psychosocial Aspects of Child and Family Health, "The Importance of Play in Promoting Healthy Child Development and Maintaining Strong Parent-Child Bonds," American Academy of Pediatrics, 10.1542/peds.2006-2697 (accessed May 1, 2018)

rooted in science. As stated by Jean Piaget, Swiss psychologist and the father of modern cognitive development studies, "Play is the work of childhood."

Before the 1930s, scientists and laypeople alike thought and taught that children were merely less sophisticated thinkers than adults. They were also believed that intelligence was not only a fixed quantity, but one determined by biology, much like complexion or eye color.

Piaget's groundbreaking work would change these opinions. He stumbled upon this line of inquiry quite by accident when in the 1920s he was charged with adapting English intelligence tests for French children.

Many of these questions involved logical thinking – a common measure of intelligence. Instead of dismissing incorrect answers as evidence of inferior cognitive skills, Piaget decided to delve deeper into the test-takers' thinking processes.

He found that intelligence is not set in stone, but an evolutionary process based on a combination of biology and life experience. This inquiry led to his theory of childhood cognitive development, which to this day remains the definitive authority in this area.[12]

Piaget's theory hinges on the idea that we all have and live

---

[12] McLeod, Saul, "Jean Paiget," Simply Psychology, https://www.simplypsychology.org/piaget.html (accessed May 1, 2018)

by a mental model of the world. This model includes "schemas" or mini scripts that we pull up from our memory banks to inform our behavior and our reasoning skills in all kinds of life situations.

When we receive new information from the world, we either use *assimilation* to fit it into our existing schemas, or *accommodation* to adjust those schemas to make room for that new knowledge.

Piaget contended that children have less life experience than adults and therefore view the world differently. Basically, they have fewer, simpler schemas. As children go through the various stages of development – and learn to assimilate and accommodate – they begin to string their experiences together.

They are building their mental models of the world, and in the process their schemas increase in number and become more complex.[13]

Piaget's theory includes four stages of development:

- Sensorimotor: from birth to 10-24 months (or until the child starts speaking)
- Preoperational: 18-24 months to seven years
- Concrete operational: seven to twelve years old

---

[13] Ibid.

- Formal operational: adolescence through

In the sensorimotor stage, the child lives in the here and now. His or her focus is on developing motor skills. Objects remain the same even when they change location. The best advantage you can give babies is to talk, read and sing to them. Teach them to play simple games like Peek-a-boo. Help them clap when you recite nursery rhythms, which will help build pre-reading patterns in the brain.

As the child enters the preconception stage, he or she begins to perceive their surroundings differently, communicate verbally and develop reasoning skills. This is a great time to take nature walks and start collections. What kid doesn't love to be chased or play make-believe with their parents?

When a child enters the intuitive stage, he or she starts to see relationships (between various objects, people, or a combination of the two), but remains unaware of the reasoning behind these relationships.

Perhaps in an attempt to understand these relationships, kids at this stage start asking a lot of questions about the world around them.

How many of us have been followed around by a curious kid asking, "Why does this thing have this part?" "Why does the swing only go so high?" "Why is the yolk yellow and the edges white in an egg?"

Children's curiosity at this stage is seemingly endless. Their limited schemas simply cannot answer all of their questions, so they are thirsty for knowledge.

Around age seven they enter the preoperational stage and begin to learn how to conserve, understand numbers, and think broadly and conceptually. They also begin to grasp the reversibility of thought and their ability to change their reasoning – these are the assimilation and accommodation skills mentioned earlier.

From ages twelve to twenty-five, they are in the formal operational stage and form the ability to deal with hypothetical and idealistic situations.[14]

Once we understand these stages, we begin to realize how important it is for children to be exposed to healthy stimulation and interaction.

During play, children construct or are introduced to scenarios and learn to solve challenges they encounter within these scenarios. In doing so they must learn to be flexible, modify their approaches when circumstances arise, and learn to roll with the punches when there is something beyond their control.

---

14 Ibid.

This holds true for everything from the mobile hanging over the infant's crib and the toddler's blocks to games for older children such as Hide & Go Seek and organized sports.

Games involving "make believe," like tea parties or cars in the sandbox, provide endless fun. These games, whether played alone or in groups, provide innumerable situations in which children can expand their worldview, learn to cope with challenges, and collaborate with others.

Playing make-believe actually helps children develop a critical cognitive skill called *executive function*. Executive function has a number of different elements, the most important of which is the ability to self-regulate. Kids with good self-regulation are able to control their emotions and behavior, resist impulses, and exhibit discipline in various social and educational situations.[15]

As discussed in the previous chapters, the ways in which children spend their free time or playtime has changed dramatically in the past two decades. There are several reasons for this change, including different parenting styles, the need for two-income households (which affects how and with whom kids spend their time), and perhaps the largest culprit, technology.

---

[15] Bodrova, Elena, Germeroth, Carrie, Leong, Deborah J., "Play and Self-Regulation: Lessons from Vygostky," American Journal of Play, http://www.journalofplay.org/issues/6/1/article/7-play-and-self-regulation-lessons-vygotsky (accessed May 1, 2018)

While the prevailing attitude has been that technological advances are good for children, a growing number of psychologists believe that they have negatively impacted kids' cognitive and emotional development.

As free play has diminished, so has children's capacity for self-regulation. In 2001, child psychologists replicated a study of self-regulation originally done in the late 1940s.

Researchers asked the participants — three-, five- and seven-year-old kids — to do a number of exercises, one of which required them to stand perfectly still. In the original study, the three-year-olds couldn't stand still at all and the five-year-olds could stand still for only about three minutes. The seven-year-olds, however, could stand there for as long as the researchers asked them to.

However, when psychologists from the Mid-Continent Research for Education and Learning repeated those exercises a half-century later, the results were quite different.

"Today's 5-year-olds were acting at the level of three-year-olds sixty years ago," stated psychologist Elena Bodrova, "and today's seven-year-olds were barely approaching the level of a five-year-old sixty years ago." She added, "So the results were very sad." [16]

---

[16] Spiegel, Alix, "The Evolution of Play," The Bryant Park Program, National Public Radio, NPR, New York, February 22, 2008.

This is an understatement, and it underscores the importance of self-regulation. Poor executive function is associated with high dropout rates, drug use and crime. In fact, good executive function is a better predictor of success in school than IQ.[17]

This goes back to Piaget's contention that intelligence is not solely rooted in – or limited by – biology, but is largely influenced by external environmental factors. Children who are able to pay attention and manage their feelings in a healthy way are better able to learn.

As executive function researcher Laura Berk explains, "Self-regulation predicts effective development in virtually every domain."[18]

According to Berk, one reason make-believe is such a powerful tool for building self-discipline is because during make-believe, children engage in something called private speech: they talk to themselves about what they are going to do and how they are going to do it.

"In fact, if we compare preschoolers' activities and the amount of private speech that occurs across them, we find

[17] Galinsky, Ellen, "Executive Function Skills Predict Children's Success in Life and in School," Huffington Post, https://www.huffingtonpost.com/ellen-galinsky/executive-function-skills_1_b_1613422.html (accessed May 1, 2018)

[18] Spiegel, Alix, "Old Fashioned Play Builds Serious Skills," Morning Edition, National Public Radio, NPR, New York February 21, 2008 https://www.npr.org/templates/story/story.php?storyId=19212514 (accessed May 1, 2018)

that this self-regulating language is highest during make-believe play," Berk says. "And this type of self-regulating language ... has been shown in many studies to be predictive of executive functions."

Children are not the only ones who use private speech to control themselves. Berk notes that as adults, "we're often using it to surmount obstacles, to master cognitive and social skills, and to manage our emotions."

Unfortunately, the more structured the play, the more children's private speech declines. Essentially, because modern children's games are so focused on lessons and leagues, and because kids' toys increasingly inhibit imaginative play, children are not getting a chance to practice policing themselves. When they do have that opportunity, says Berk, the results are clear: self-regulation improves.

One index that researchers, including myself, have used is the extent to which a child, for example, cleans up independently after a free-choice period in preschool. We find that children who are most effective at complex make-believe play take on that responsibility with greater willingness, and even will assist others in doing so without teacher prompting.

Yet, despite the body of evidence on the benefits of imaginative play, it continues to decline, even when it comes to preschool-age children. According to Yale psychological researcher Dorothy Singer, teachers and school administrators just don't see the value.

Because of the testing, and the emphasis now that you have to really pass these tests, teachers are starting earlier and earlier to drill the kids in their basic fundamentals. Play is viewed as unnecessary, a waste of time. I have so many articles that have documented the shortening of free play for children, where the teachers in these schools are using the time for cognitive skills.[19]

It seems that in the rush to give children every advantage – to protect them, to stimulate them and to enrich them – our culture has unwittingly compromised one of the activities that helped children most. As it turns out, all that "wasted" play time was not such a waste after all.

Let's not forget another critical point: play for play's sake is also a child's purest form of enjoyment; whether it's Duck, Duck, Goose or Tag. These games mold our children's lives and worldview.

Following are some of my favorite childhood indoor games. Also fun to play outside, especially with a bunch of rambunctious boys.

---

[19] Ibid.

Crash Up Derby

All players gather in a circle about twenty feet in diameter (after removing sharp objects like end tables so as to avoid bumps on heads and bodies).

The players get down on their knees with arms behind their backs and hands held together. The object is to belly bump or side bump or head jam another player off their knees or out of the circle. If a player is knocked down or out of the arena they have to sit out and chant encouragement to the remaining players.

Crash Up Derby not only promotes balance and physical stamina, but helps players learn to think strategically. Each child has to size up the others, discern who is the strongest, and then recruit others to double- or triple-team them.

Once the strongest player is out, the alliance ends and it becomes winner-take-all. The game continues until everyone is worn out and ready for a drink or snack.

It is an excellent learning experience in healthy competition and collaboration.

Knots Landing

Here is an activity that really ties people together.

At least five players stand in a small circle and place their right hands out in front of them, thumbs up. With the left hand, each grabs someone else's thumb, but not that of anyone next to him or her.

The object of this activity is to untangle this knot by stepping over, crawling under, or turning around. Anything that will unravel the knot is allowed except letting go.

If the players really get into dead-end situation, they can always apply "knot aid" by allowing one player let go and untangle. Then the remaining players join hands again.

Don't let them give up too easily: most knots can be untangled with a little patience and plenty of togetherness.

Don't let two players grab one another's hands. That will simply allow two people to stand around and get in the way as everyone else tried to untangle the knot.

CHAPTER 4

RECEDING RECESS

At the time of this writing, the United States was mourning the casualties resulting from the latest in a long line of devastating school shootings. As always happens in the aftermath of such travesties, everyone from parents and mental health professionals to gun control advocates and journalists tried to parse what happened in Broward County, Florida.[20]

While we may never know all the reasons why a specific attack occurred, their increasing frequency leaves no doubt that they share an underlying theme of social isolation, hopelessness, and an inability to connect to others in a healthy way.

---

[20] Detman, Gary, "Sheriff: 17 dead, gunman in custody in shooting at Florida high school," CBS12, http://cbs12.com/news/local/shooting-at-marjory-stoneman-douglas-high-school-in-parkland (accessed May 1, 2018)

We know this, yet we continue to keep moving in the wrong direction, particularly the way in which we (mis)manage our children's play.

As mentioned earlier, free play, whether indoors or outdoors, encourages and nurtures fellowship, cooperation and diplomacy among its players. In other words, it fosters the kind of support system so many of our children are lacking these days.

This is not to suggest that more playtime would prevent shootings or other attacks, but the elimination of it may certainly be a contributing factor to the climate of fear and violence pervading our schools today.

Even as organic free play has decreased over the past several decades, kids could still count on getting some play time during the school day. Who does not remember squirming in class, counting the minutes until the bell rang for recess? We got to toss a ball around, play Foursquare, or just run wild, releasing mental and physical energy before buckling down for the rest of our classes.

Unfortunately, increasingly rigorous academic curricula, as well as a need to control every moment of our children's lives in a misguided attempt to foster "success," has led to an erosion of this most valuable experience.

While this is an international issue, it seems to be particularly prevalent in the U.S. This is due, at least in part, to the rigid demands of federal and state "consequential accountability statutes" that among other things, tie school funding to standardized test scores.[21]

Teachers feel pressured to cut down on recreational time in favor of more class time and homework. While the resulting academic improvement is questionable and dependent on a multitude of factors, we do know that keeping children from free play is hampering their creativity, as well as their ability to relate to each other and to their physical environment.

The importance of recess and its gradual disappearance from our kids' lives has not gone unnoticed. In the 1980s, American children had two or three sessions of recess a day; now they average one session amounting to less than a half hour – barely enough time to complete a game and probably not long enough to experience and resolve conflict in any meaningful way.

However, as illustrated by James Mollison, British author of the book *Playground*, it does not have to be this way. As Mollison travelled to various schools around the world, his intent was simply to study the various ways in which kids play during their school breaks; he also wound up shedding light

---

[21] Fair Test, "No Time for Recess, No Need for Nap," Fair Test: The National Center for Fair and Open Testing," https://fairtest.org/no-time-recess-no-need-nap (accessed May 1, 2018)

on how other countries still utilize recess as a valuable tool for learning – physically, mentally and socially.

The ideas about recess are as varied as the countries themselves.[22]

In Japan, kids not only have longer official recess times, but ten-to-fifteen-minute breaks each hour.

Chinese children do not have free-play time, but they do have a morning exercise break, as well as exercise time for their eyes (they move their eyes to music to reduce fatigue and increase concentration).

In Finland, recess more closely resembled that of American schools but for a much longer period – 75 minutes on average.[23]

Perhaps the most impressive example of recess was in Norway. There, children go outside to play, no matter whether it's sunny or in the middle of a snowstorm.

The playgrounds are populated with trees, rocks and sticks, and the children are permitted to climb *as high as they want* and build whatever their minds can conceive of and their bodies have the strength for.

---

[22] Sanchez, Gabriel, H., "This is What Recess Looks Like Around the World," Buzz Feed, https://www.buzzfeed.com/gabrielsanchez/this-is-what-recess-looks-like-around-the-world?utm_term=.npEJAVZxq#.edMlD1mqZ (accessed May 1, 2018)

[23] Ibid.

They are also expected to resolve any disputes that arise among them, and unless there is a serious problem (i.e., bullying), the teacher will not interfere.

This sort of unfettered play is unimaginable in the vast majority of American schools.[24]

Many child experts believe that decreased play is at least partly to blame for the near-epidemic number of Attention Deficit Hyperactivity Disorder (ADHD) diagnoses among American children. While there are other factors involved, it is no coincidence that in the 1970s, when free play was a natural part of life, ADHD was a rare condition, affecting about 1 percent of schoolchildren.

As of 2012, 11 percent (more than one in ten) had been diagnosed with this disorder. Since then, this number has continued to climb, and with it, the numbers of prescriptions for drugs like Ritalin and Adderall.[25]

Today, millions of American children are taking these drugs, sometimes for years. While these drugs can be safe and effective when one has a legitimate diagnosis and uses them as directed, they are also potentially addictive, and the long-term effects on young minds are not fully known.

---

[24] Ibid.

[25] Schwarz, Alan and Cohen, Sarah, "A.D.H.D. Seen in 11% of U.S. Children as Diagnoses Rise," New York Times, https://www.nytimes.com/2013/04/01/health/more-diagnoses-of-hyperactivity-causing-concern.html (accessed May 1, 2018)

We do know that with prolonged use, such drugs alter the pleasure centers of the brain, making it more difficult to feel joy at daily things such as spending time with loved ones. This can lead to depression and abuse of other substances.

We know these things, yet doctors, educators and even parents continue to bury their heads in the sand, often forgoing organic treatments like counseling and behavioral modification in favor of pills and more restrictive schedules.

While some children have been accurately diagnosed, there are certainly many who would benefit from simple lifestyle changes. For example, sunlight has been proven to reduce the symptoms of ADHD and possibly even prevent it; proponents of this theory point to the lower number of diagnoses in states with a lot of sunlight.[26]

Researchers are still gaining more insight about the detrimental effects of young peoples' increasing amounts of screen time. In 2018, USC and UCLA conducted a study of 2,500 high school students that showed, "On average, with each notch a teen climbed up the scale of digital engagement, his or her average level of reported ADHD symptoms rose by about 10 percent."[27]

---

[26] Deans, Emily, M.D., "Sunlight and ADHD: Evidence that bright sunlight can ameliorate symptoms of ADHD," Psychology Today, https://www.psychologytoday.com/us/blog/evolutionary-psychiatry/201304/sunlight-and-adhd (May 1, 2018)

[27] Healy, M. (2018, July 19). Study: Teens' Screen Time Links to ADHD. *Missoulian*, p. A4.

This kind of finding cannot be ignored; parents must take more responsibility for the time their children spend zoning out in front of a screen.

Almost more alarming is this finding from psychologist Jean M. Twenge, who "found dissatisfaction highest among those who spent the most time locked onto a screen. As time spent in offline activities increased, so did happiness."[28]

Adolescents will need a lot of parental encouragement to seek out fun offline activities. If parents can get their children engaged in a sport or other extracurricular at a young age, they may be able to combat the siren call of the screen, as well as the negative effects they produce.

Parents need to help their children enjoy athletic participation, including signing them up for organized sports. However, they must be mindful not to push their kids too hard. The following account is from a man whose daughter excelled in softball, only to end her career prematurely because of the constant pressure placed on her by adults.

It began when she was only eight years old and playing for the first time. Though the score wasn't kept on the field, parents in the stands kept an unofficial tally, while cheering, "Come on, we're ahead" and yelling jeers of "Easy out!" when a poorly skilled player came to bat.

---

[28] Ibid.

Just two years later, the father noticed that parents and coaches wanted to up the ante considerably, with their focus shifting from fun to preparing the girls for the "next level" of competition.

That meant taking a fun, highly anticipated seasonal game and making it a year-round commitment complete with regular, rigorous practices and preseason games.

Players would now be expected to be in the gym throughout the off-season, and that was just for one sport! If the girls had other interests, their lives would be that much more consumed.

The girl's father soon found himself caught up in it. "We thought, if we don't choose the same path for our child, she would be left behind … She wouldn't make Varsity in high school, which meant she wouldn't make a college team. Then certainly a scholarship would be out the window as well."

Once you start thinking this way, he noted, things tend to take on a life of their own. Soon the family was traveling long distances for tournaments, and while there were fun aspects, the underlying pressure to play "at the next level" was always lurking beneath the surface.

Ironically, the constant practice and, year-round drumbeat of *go, go, go* eventually led to his daughter's complete burnout. She was a top player and a very skilled athlete; college coaches attended the tournaments and "scouted" her, offering her the scholarships everyone coveted, but by then the fun was gone.

The father now admits that he and his wife didn't realize how much pressure they had been putting on her. Now he advocates that parents let kids enjoy the game for the purpose it was intended ... a *game*.

As I mentioned earlier, one of my mom's favorite childhood games was "Red Light, Green Light." Below is the variation of the game that my friends and I enjoyed as kids.

It's a great opportunity to get outside and expel physical energy while learning strategy and healthy competition.

Red Light, Green Light

Like many of activities from my childhood, this game is highly inclusive – anyone, regardless of gender or age could play. You can also include as many participants as you like, as long as you have at least three to start the game. To begin, an area is designated as "The Kingdom" and one player is chosen as the King. The King will go stand at the front of the "Kingdom," while the other players stand at the end of the play on the periphery – or "Moat."

Their goal: to gain entry into the Kingdom and capture the King. The King faces the players in the Moat and starts by proclaiming "Red Light!!" During red light, the players in the Moat are not allowed to move.

The King then turns his or her back to the Moat and calls out "Green Light!" During green light the players attempting to capture the King advance, trying to get close as possible before the King turns back and yells "Red Light!" once again. Once he or she does, they all have to be perfectly still. If the King sees anyone moving at all, that player must return to the Moat and start over.

Players can be on their knees, stomach, or feet as long as there is enough room. The play continues, usually with much laughter and denials about who had really been seen moving, until a player gets close enough to touch the King.

The length of each Red Light and Green Light period is up to the King, who can shorten or lengthen them in order to fool the approaching players.

When the King is captured, the player who first reaches the Kingdom becomes the new King, and the previous King is sent to the Moat.

The game is repeated over and over, and it is a fun way for everyone to play together and enjoy strategizing about how to capture the King.

CHAPTER 5

HELICOPTER PARENTS AND HEAD GAMES:
A LESSON IN FORCED PLAY

Throughout this book, we have discussed the decline of free play in our society and the damaging effects it has on our youth. There are several reasons for this, including a greater reliance on technology and shorter recess periods at school. Underscoring this phenomenon is a nearly obsessive "hands-on" approach on the part of parents.[29]

While so-called "helicopter parenting" has gained a lot of media attention in recent years, the term was actually coined by Dr. Haim Ginott in his 1969 book, *Parents & Teenagers.*

Since then, over-parenting has become much more common, in part because both parents now work outside the home. They feel guilty for not spending more time with their

---

[29] Carlson, Melinda, "10 Warning Signs that You Might Be a Helicopter Parent (And How to Stop)," A Fine Parent, https://afineparent.com/be-positive/helicopter-parent.html (accessed May 1, 2018)

children and over-compensate by micromanaging every aspect of their youngsters' lives.

While "helicopter parenting" manifests itself in many ways, the underlying reason is always fear. These parents fear their child will get injured, so they control the physical environment as much as possible.

These parents fear their child will be emotionally wounded or "walked all over," so they insert themselves into his or her disputes with other children, even to the extent of calling the parents and negotiating a truce.

Perhaps most of all, they fear becoming like their *own* parents. If they grew up in a very rigid home with lots of chores, they never ask their kids to wash the dishes or make their beds; the children may not even face consequences when they misbehave.

If their parents didn't show much interest in their education, helicopter parents will obsess over their own child's academic performance, pushing them to take this or that class, and sometimes even doing homework for them!

Unfortunately, these well-meaning mothers and fathers are rendering their children incapable of navigating life. By the time they get to college, those raised by helicopter parents are often underperforming in their studies. Later on, these problems often extend to careers and even affect their social skills and physical fitness.

Free play has also been a casualty of helicopter parenting. Overworked parents often lack the time to throw a ball around with their kids. Or, as such parents are prone to do, they keep a careful eye on their kids' playtime with others.

Some parents feel the best way to help their child is to place him or her in a pay-to-play program that is organized and coached by adults. These parents want their children to reap the benefits of physical activity and being part of a team. Many also recognize that extracurricular activities look good on college applications, and figure they will kill two birds with one stone.

What they fail to recognize, however, is that organized sports programs, while an excellent supplement to free play, are not a replacement for it.

The spontaneity and joy of practicing without worrying about making mistakes – or better yet, laughing about those mistakes – are what makes such play so important. Once kids become part of an official organization, they are subject to rules, not of their own making, but enforced by the adults around them.

They are also assigned teams, rather than learning to choose their own. Moreover, when disputes arise, they learn to rely on a third-party (the adult) to lay down the law, rather than figuring out the best solution for themselves. Thus, they are not allowed to learn valuable life lessons: problem solving, cooperation, negotiation and playing fair.

Parents are becoming more cognizant of the pressure they place on their children, particularly with regard to organized sports.

One such person is Steve Resner, whose overzealous attempts to "help" his son excel in baseball resulted in a great strain on their relationship.

It must be said that Steve, who in high school was a state champion wrestler and a Greco-Roman Exchange athlete, is also a caring and wonderful person who tries to help everyone he encounters.

Like most parents, he only had the best of intentions but fell into the all-too common trap of helicopter parenting. The account below details his personal experience and how he came to realize that sometimes less is more when it comes to facilitating our children's success, and happiness.

"To be honest, I don't know when the shift from celebrating my son's successes to measuring and comparing his successes began.

I cannot pinpoint an age or an event when my expectations (or, more accurately, my hopes and dreams) for my son started to drive me, and therefore drive him, on a path where sports and his success at them became an obsession.

"I just know that somewhere along the line, I went from

delight at watching five-year-olds kick each other in the shins on the soccer field to shouting out comments, like 'Why are you not hustling?'; 'Why didn't you pass the ball?'; 'Why are you letting that kid run past you?'; and 'Come on, buddy, you're better than these kids!'

"This mentality escalated when my son started playing baseball. I noticed early on that while other children were fiddling with their mitts and worrying about what snack was going to be provided, my son was actually hitting and fielding the ball and showing true talent for the game.

That's where the drive for participation, competition and perfection really began. I became obsessed with the idea that he could truly excel; before I knew it, I was sure a college scholarship and perhaps even a career in baseball was in his future.

"Baseball transitioned from, *Let's go play catch and hit some balls, buddy,* to demanding each evening that he work on his game. Major red flag, folks: if, after a game of catch or a sporting event, you and your son go home frustrated, you have not played with – or supported – him.

"By the time he was nine or ten, my son's participation and success in baseball had become the center of my world. I shifted time and money from other family activities and focused instead on searching for the right travel teams, the right teammates, the right group of parents and the right environment to showcase his talents.

"Worst of all, I appointed myself his coach and manager and placed my most important role – as his dad – on the backburner.

"What was lost to me – and ultimately, my son – was the joy that I had experienced as a kid participating in sports. I grew up playing with my friends, and my parents celebrated my being on any team, and any success I/we had was a bonus.

"I was able to discover my own talents and choose the sports that I felt were a good fit for me. I was in high school before I ever stepped foot on a wrestling mat and was still awarded a scholarship to the University of Montana.

At no time was my participation in sports demanded; the only requirement was that once I committed to a sport I had to stick it out for the season.

"Today, in the ultra-competitive sports environment that we parents have created, we have lost the knowledge that a ten-year-old does not need a personal trainer. We have forgotten that playing with your friends is *not* the same as competing with your teammates.

We have misplaced the awareness that it is truly okay if a child is not scheduled ten to twelve hours a day, six or seven day a week.

"Unlike my son, I was not forced onto structured travel teams and into an environment hell-bent on assembling the ultimate win-loss record.

"I would also be remiss not to mention the substantial amount of money that was spent (squandered) over ten-plus years in search of the ultimate baseball camp or tournament, with its elusive promise that a college scout would be present or a scholarship obtained. Let's face it – these places and events are moneymakers for people who want us to believe the illusion that our child is the .01%.

"At the end of the day, what was missing in my life was balance. While I don't believe all of my efforts were a waste, a great deal of this money and time could have been spent on vacations that created lasting memories for the family or set aside for actual future college expenses instead of weekend events that became a job my son never wanted.

"Sports should have been a piece of his development, not the priority. He once tried to tell me this, saying he needed a break and that baseball ultimately didn't and wouldn't matter, but it fell on deaf ears. As a consequence of my behavior, we missed out on other activities, such as fishing, hunting, or just having conversations that did not center on his batting average. That's something I regret to this day.

"By his senior year of high school the relationship between my son and I had become a battle, with me relentlessly pushing him to play and him trying desperately to remove the cancer that baseball had become from his life. Ultimately, my son walked away from baseball and the negativity that came with it, both on the field and in our home.

"Hindsight, as they say, is twenty-twenty, so the least I can do is share the value of my hindsight with other fathers. Let your child lead the way when it comes to sports. If it's important to them they will let you know.

"Let your child explore everything; your job is to provide experiences and tools but resist the urge to push them in any one direction. If your child asks you to throw the ball or to help them work on their swing, remember if you don't have fun, you've failed.

"Remind yourself that you are the dad, not their coach or manager, and, finally, never sacrifice your relationship with your child for a dream, a stat or a win."

Steve's experience provides a valuable lesson for parents who, despite their best intentions, may be projecting their own needs for glory onto their children. In allowing kids to make their own choices about sports, parents are validating and supporting their child's voice in all areas of life. And, as difficult as this may be for some parents to accept, this includes allowing children to make the "wrong" choices, fail, and learn from their mistakes.

This issue has even caught the attention of professional sports organizations such as the National Football League (NFL). In 2007, the NFL launched a Play-60 campaign. They urged parents to make sure their children unplug from computers and cell phones and engage in real play for at least 60 minutes a day.

The campaign's stated mission was to fight childhood obesity and foster a lifelong commitment to physical fitness, while recognizing other benefits of play such as fostering healthy social skills and face-to-face relationships.

The NFL also recognizes that children will not be interested in sports if they don't learn to enjoy playing them for fun.

I coached and administered a youth touch football camp in Missoula for 20 years (from 1997 to 2017) called Little Grizzly Football FUNdamental camp. The camp focused on teaching youth the basic skills of football. We taught the proper techniques of throwing, running, kicking, blocking, form tackling, game strategy and offered games every day for the participants.

We also had local college football players help teach the players as role models and tell stories of how they learned the game and why they enjoyed the experience of the sport in their lives.

The camp was very popular as we also had local high

school and college football coaches, and even current NFL pros that were home for the summer, stop by to give demonstrations and tell stories to the campers.

What amazed me every year was how the participants loved the camp and the parents mentioned at the end of the camp how sad the campers were that it was ending. It dawned on me that the players didn't play touch football in their local neighborhoods like I did when I was a child and they yearned for the free play opportunity that our camp provided.

I always mentioned to the participants to look for the chance to find other people where they lived and form play groups for touch football games outside in parks, even with only four, six, or eight other players.

One event at camp that we offered every year was a race day where the campers would race to see what grade level players were fastest, i.e., first graders, second graders and so on. Then we would see if the fastest campers could beat the local high school or college coaches in the camp.

After we established which college football camp coach was fastest they would "race" my Labrador retriever Gypsie in a 60-yard dash to see if the college player was faster than the retriever.

I would have the campers pick a sideline and go to the sideline for the player if they thought the player would win the 60-yard dash, or go to the other sideline if they thought the Labrador would win the race. By the way, the player racing would get the advantage of a running start.

My son would hold the dog at the starting line, as I would wait 60 yards away and call out, "On your mark, get set, GO!"

The player would get a 10-yard starting sprint and off he would come toward me full tilt as the players lining the sidelines screamed out encouragement. The winner got camp bragging rights, and the losing sideline of players had to do 30 military style push-ups.

You would have thought the winners were getting a million dollars in prize money as the screams grew louder and louder during the race. Well, Gypsie retired a champion, being undefeated for all the years she raced the college players, expect the final year she lost by a nose (because I dropped the football I was holding).

The point of this event and the camp was the fun that was had by the participants. Everyone loved this event and their whole experience. The local paper even covered it one year.

It is the fun from this kind of play, and from being with each other, that I worry is missing in today's digital world. Especially because our smartphone technology-based experiences require no human interaction or discussion.

Another benefit that the participants in our camp realized

firsthand was how practice improved their skill level immediately. Their parents got to witness that firsthand, too.

The campers' skill increased simply from warm-ups – catching a football from a further distance – 10 to 20 to 30 yards – as the camp progressed. They also became faster, better runners who could even run backwards and sideways, and their bounce-up speeds from our up-down drills improved daily.

We conducted tests at the close of camp for strength (push-ups and sit-ups), running, throwing, kicking and leg lifts. All of these skills had improved during the four-day camp. The top performers in each grade level of each skill were recognized, and the parents got to witness the proud faces of the campers as they received their awards.

I believe the lessons the campers learned from the stories the coaches shared and the skills they improved upon made a real difference in their lives. These experiences helped each camper acknowledge that hard work and participation in sports can be fun and beneficial.

CHAPTER 6

PLAYING IT SAFE

The previous chapter mentioned the fears of helicopter parents with regard to their children's safety – and some of the detrimental ways in which they manage those fears.

That said, they do have some very valid justifications for feeling the way they do.

The world is a far less trusting place than it was when we were children.

People are more transient – they move around the country in search of better jobs and quality of life, and therefore don't form the same loyalty to their neighbors, if they even know their neighbors at all.

Children, regardless of their race, religion, or socioeconomic status, face the very real perils of both "stranger danger" and violence at the hands of their classmates.

The Internet arguably contributes to this climate of fear. For one, we have access to the twenty-four-hour news cycle, the vast majority of which carries the message of doom and gloom.

If one news outlet breaks a story of a child kidnapping, you can bet every other outlet will focus on that story as well, giving the impression that such occurrences are much more prevalent than they truly are.

The digital world is also a haven for predators, who pose as other youths with the intent of luring children to meet them in real life. Yet despite this, parents seem less likely to restrict their child's access to Facebook than they do to a grassy field a block from home.

There are also some legitimate risks associated with organized sports such as football. These risks have largely been deemed "acceptable" to some extent – just ask any *Friday Night Lights* fan, who sat glued to their TV as quarterback Jason Street suffered a spinal cord injury during a game.

That was not the show's finale, but its pilot episode, a tragic event that set the tone for the next several seasons. No one suggested the Dillon Panthers stop playing the game, but highlighted their indomitable spirit and commitment to the team and to their community.

In recent years, however, other risks have begun to emerge about football, prompting the NFL to make a long overdue admission that may very well lead to an overhaul of American football.

A 2017 Boston University study revealed that out of 111 subjects, all former NFL players, 110 showed signed of Chronic Traumatic Encephalopathy (CTE), a devastating neurodegenerative disease resulting from multiple head injuries.

The symptoms, which include changes in mood and behavioral problems, often don't appear until years after those injuries occurred.

These symptoms and behaviors are also irreversible and can lead to violence, dementia and death.[30]

CTE, specifically its connection to tackle football, was originally brought to light in a 2005 paper published by Bennet Ifeakandu Omalu, a Nigerian-American doctor, forensic pathologist and neuropathologist based in Pennsylvania.

Dr. Omalu's research on CTE originated with his 2002 autopsy of former Pittsburgh Steelers player Mike Webster, who died suddenly after years of

---

[30] Perez, A.J., "New Boston University study links repetitive hits to head, not concussions, to CTE," USA Today, https://www.usatoday.com/story/sports/2018/01/18/boston-university-study-repetitive-hits-head-not-concussions-cte/1043489001/ (accessed May 1, 2018)

cognitive, behavioral, and mood problems, as well as substance abuse and suicide attempts.[31]

Formerly, CTE had been associated mainly with professional boxers; however, Omalu's work led to the revelations of a long list of NFL players who suffered from dementia and/or committed violence against others. Several had ended their own lives.

One example was Terry Long, another former NFL player who had killed himself at age 45. The autopsy revealed that Long's brain had some of the same characteristics as a 90-year-old with Alzheimer's.

Omalu published those findings in 2006; however, it would take another ten years and much debate before the NFL admitted, before Congress, that they believed there was a connection between the game and CTE.

It probably didn't hurt that in 2015, Will Smith played Dr. Omalu in the film *Concussion*, for which he received several award nominations.

In 2017, the autopsy of Aaron Hernandez revealed that he too had severe CTE. The 27-year-old former tight end for the New England Patriots, who had a long history of arrests, killed himself after being tried for three murders, one of

[31] Breslow, Jason, M. "The Autopsy that Changed Football," Frontline, PBS, October 6, 2013 https://www.pbs.org/wgbh/frontline/article/the-autopsy-that-changed-football/ (accessed May 1, 2018)

which he was convicted.[32]

These horrifying incidents have given rise to a push, both inside and outside the NFL, to change to flag football, a version in which a player removes a flag from the ball carrier's belt, rather than tackling him.

Some argue that this would reduce the risk of CTE, while others claim that better headgear would be just as effective. Still others approach the issue from a "purist" standpoint, arguing that players go into the game knowing the risks (as well as the hope of fame and fortune) just as fans go to the stadium expecting the excitement of traditional tackle football.

Though the future of professional football is unclear, major changes seem likely, if only to protect the incoming generations of players.

The risk-versus-reward argument loses all merit when it comes to CTE's countless other victims. Of the estimated 5.5 million Americans aged six and over who played tackle football in 2017, only a tiny fraction will even get close to the NFL, yet they too are at grave risk of the degenerative brain disease.

The same Boston University study noted above also found

[32] Einbinder, Nicole, "Aaron Hernandez Found to Have Had 'Severe' Case of CTE," Frontline, PBS, September 21, 2017, https://www.pbs.org/wgbh/frontline/article/aaron-hernandez-found-to-have-had-severe-case-of-cte/ (accessed May 1, 2018)

that three of fourteen high school players and forty-eight of fifty-three college players had CTE. The fact that they didn't play as long or as hard did not protect them from its life-altering, and often life-ending, effects.[33]

Neither, it seems, will helmets. Equipment prevents skulls fractures, "but the head still moves around inside the helmet," stated Dr. Robert Stern, neuropsychologist and co-director of Boston University's Center for the Study of Traumatic Encephalopathy, "and the brain, more importantly, still moves around inside the skull. That's what causes brain trauma."[34]

In 2011, Peter Grant, a 49-year-old accountant and media consultant, hung himself in his garage. Grant had played football and hockey in high school, during which he sustained at least seven concussions, and then went on to play intermural sports at Notre Dame. That was back in the early 1980s.

Flash forward to 2009, when the kind, once happy husband and father began toggling between depression and violent outbursts of anger. After his death his widow donated

[33] Freyer, Felice, J. "CTE can begin soon after head injury, even in teens, BU study finds," Boston Globe, https://www.bostonglobe.com/metro/2018/01/18/cte-can-begin-soon-after-head-injury-even-teens-study-finds/yApExpCyyiESvgOYviI6NK/story.html (accessed May 1, 2018)

[34] Kristof, Nicholas, "Veterans and Brain Disease," The New York Times, https://www.nytimes.com/2012/04/26/opinion/kristof-veterans-and-brain-disease.html (accessed May 1, 2018)

his brain to Boston University Medical Center, where it was determined that he had CTE.

Spurred in part by the NFL's admission of the link between football and CTE, more and more high schools are switching to flag football. According to a 2017 *Huffington Post* article, it is the fastest growing sport among American youth, particularly young children.

In the summer of 2017, a new groundbreaking study, "DIAGNOSE CTE," began at Boston University Medical Center. Over the next seven years a team comprised of experts from across the country will study the brain scans and biomarkers of 240 men in the hopes of developing ways to diagnose CTE in the living.

The subjects are aged 45 to 74; half are former NFL players; 60 played college football; and the remaining 60 never seriously played any contact sport.

While as of yet there is no cure for CTE, the hope is that early diagnosis can aid in the management of symptoms, and perhaps eventually the ability the halt the disease.[35]

While problems of the world – whether in stadiums or in backyards – may seem insurmountable, there are in fact some

---

[35] Almendrala, Anna, "Scientists May Be On The Way To Developing A Test For CTE," Huffington Post, https://www.huffingtonpost.com/entry/cte-diagnose-test_us_59ca984be4b07e9ca11f3877 (accessed May 1, 2018)

simple steps we can take to make things safer – and more fun – for our children.

When it comes to local free play, two key words are *connectedness* and *grassroots*, meaning people need to come together to play face-to-face and on a local level, in order to start building trusting relationships.

Many areas have neighborhood watches, in which citizens get together to help deter crime. If we can find the time to prevent something undesirable from happening, why can't we get together to bring about something beneficial?

Imagine, for example, a group of people – kids and adults – who get together and play some game or sport together. Playing with others, especially those of other generations, has many positive aspects: people learn from one another, witness each other's pure enjoyment of the game, and offer mutual support and encouragement.

In doing so, both kids and adults can relieve stress, form new bonds of friendship and establish trust. If necessary, parents can rotate in and out of the activities as their work schedules dictate.

In between the group get-togethers, children who might never have met otherwise can engage in more spontaneous free play. Kids who succeed in school and life have a group of friends and playmates they can count on and trust.

CHAPTER 7

PLAY FOR ADULTS

"We don't stop playing because we grow old; we grow old because we stop playing." Though Nobel Prize-winning playwright George Bernard Shaw died nearly 70 years ago, his words are just as relevant today. They were also eerily prescient of the fast-paced, work-obsessed world we live in today.

Adults in their thirties and forties are primarily concerned with building their careers and earning enough to support their families. That often means getting up at the crack of dawn, a stressful commute either in their own car or public transportation, and then sitting behind a desk, typing away on a computer.

Other than hurried bites of a sandwich for lunch, there is usually little time to relax or replenish themselves. At the end of the day they reverse the commute, and after eating dinner and perhaps doing some household chores, they plop down on the couch to "wind down" before having to do it all again the next day.

Weekends are taken up largely with errands or other obligations, and before they know it they're doing nothing for personal enjoyment. Over time, they forget what fun even is; their bodies feel old and their minds sluggish.

This is the sort of lifestyle Shaw warned us against, and since he lived to age 94 and was a prolific writer until the year before he died, it's safe to assume he offered sound advice.

Play is just as critical for adults as it is for children, and for mainly the same reasons: it fosters creativity and imagination and assists in problem-solving and analytical thinking.

Active play also releases endorphins, which leads to a sense of well-being and improves brain function, especially when one plays games like chess and puzzles.

This helps keep the mind agile and as people age, can maintain stamina, confidence, and even help prevent dementia.[36]

Adult play also has several social benefits. Just as children are learning how to navigate the world in relation to others,

---

[36] HelpGuide.Org, "The Benefits of Play for Adults: How Play Benefits Your Relationships, Job, Bonding, and Mood," https://www.helpguide.org/articles/mental-health/benefits-of-play-for-adults.htm (accessed May 1, 2018)

adults need to be reminded of how to do these things.

Most people have several complex relationships they must maintain: with their significant others, coworkers, neighbors and children. Over time, stress from hectic schedules and the demands of everyday life can lead to disputes and resentment, even with those closest to us.

Play helps us build trust, resolve disputes and clear up emotional debris. It also helps us set healthy boundaries and break down walls based on socioeconomic, ethnic or political differences. It can even break the ice on a first date or at party where a lot of guests don't know each other.

As mentioned in previous chapters, unstructured play is critical to achieve the types of benefits mentioned above.

This includes things like tossing a ball around with some friends, playing tag with your kids or running in the park with your dog; it can be any activity you enjoy, as long as you play with abandon and your only goal is to enjoy the experience.

Right now you might be thinking, I can't remember the last time I saw my friends for a beer, let alone scheduled a game of toss. The first thing I would say is that you don't have the time *not* to engage in play, for it is something that will enhance and prolong your mental and physical health.

The second thing is that there are many other ways to weave play into your everyday schedule. Believe it or not, this includes your job.

Google is known to be one of the best companies in the world to work for; in fact, as of 2017 it has topped Fortune's Best 100 Companies list six years in a row. On any typical day, Google employees can be found exercising in the onsite gym, walking dogs – their own or their coworkers' – playing ping-pong, bowling or taking a yoga class.

Google execs understand that when you give employees ample time to rejuvenate their minds, bodies and spirits, they will have higher morale, more productivity and far less burnout and turnover.

Also, just as negative work experiences tend to carry over into one's personal life, happy employees will be generally happier and healthier in all aspects. Everyone benefits.[37]

If you own your own business or are in a position to influence the culture at your job, you might want to think about incorporating regular play into your workplace, or encourage employees to do so.

This can be as simple as introducing a fun puzzle at a meeting, thereby promoting teamwork and a feeling of connectedness, or giving your employees "recess" times throughout the day, especially when working on a challenging project.

[37] Yang, Lucy, "13 incredible perks of working at Google, according to employees," Insider, http://www.thisisinsider.com/coolest-perks-of-working-at-google-in-2017-2017-7 (accessed May 1, 2018)

If you set the tone that you care about and respect those who work for you, they will reward you with their loyalty and their best work. If you are not in a position to set rules, you can still find ways to incorporate some aspect of play into your workday. This can be as simple as joking with coworkers, or perhaps organizing a brisk walk during lunch.

There are other ways for adults to incorporate play into their lives. You can arrange for game nights with friends; these can be indoor games such as cards or charades, or outdoor games, such as Tag, Hide and Go Seek, or volleyball. It all depends on the time of year and the area in which you live.

If your usual crowd won't get in on the fun, make some new friends. Meetup.com is an online platform that connects people of similar interests within a certain geographical area.

You need only create a profile, click on the activities you enjoy or would like to try – be it painting, hiking, hand-gliding, et cetera – and you will receive emails with new groups popping up. If there are no groups in your area that reflect your interests, you can start your own meetup.

Of course, one of the best ways to play is with children, whether they are yours, a grandchild, a niece or nephew, et cetera. Set aside some time to give them your undivided attention (be sure to shut off or silence your phone!) and let them lead the way.

There is much you can learn from a child with regard to play, no matter their age. They will remind you what it is like to play in a creative, unstructured way, using the objects at hand or just your imagination.

CONCLUSION

My primary purpose in writing this book was to discuss the many benefits of free play; the decline in such play over the past several decades; and to inform parents and other caretakers how they might reintroduce play into their children's daily lives.

As you may have guessed, however, this book is not just a guide about the mechanics of childhood recreation, but a commentary on our society and the vast changes, whether positive or negative, it has undergone during my lifetime.

As my dear friend Mike McChesney wrote in the foreword, we grew up in a simpler – and some would argue, happier – time. We felt safe, both in a physical sense and in our ability to create our world and ourselves.

We were also, within the confines of "make believe," able

to develop healthy relationships with others. In other words, we were free to be *children* – carefree and able to explore endless potentialities before taking on the responsibilities of "real life."

Unstructured play, in large part, both reflected and reinforced that society. The games at the end of each chapter, for example, are not only fun, they are microcosms of life – players make choices both as individuals and as members of a team, hopefully for the betterment of both.

That is not to say we always won; in fact, losing was an integral part of the learning process and quite possibly the more valuable experience.

Losing helped us to see what we were really made of. In learning humility, we learned the difference between confidence and arrogance. We learned to be gracious, and not to pity others, but to respect them.

Winning and losing is a part of daily life, no matter what career, relationship or game you are playing. Games and fun activities formed our character and helped us to play as a team.

Today, our culture seems to be moving in another direction. Somewhere along the line, we decided that "achievement" was more important the happiness, that being "connected" to the global community was more important than connecting with the person living next door.

Children are constantly monitored, policed and molded according to what adults believe is the most direct route to "success" as defined by current mores. They are encouraged to circumvent natural development and instead learn how to score highest on a standardized test or to best a computer game, rather than learn healthy competition with others.

In addition to pushing children to excel, many are also protected in such a way that "helicopter parents" fear normal friendships and neighborhood groups.

Without actively meaning to isolate their children, latchkey kids are told to stay inside where they will be "safe." The children's best friends thus become the television, game console and computer.

That said, it is my primary goal not to argue against progress, but to begin to integrate it with some of the values and simple pleasures that seem to have fallen by the wayside.

Finally, it is my sincerest wish that those who read this book will not only make fun a priority for their children, but a lifelong pursuit for themselves.

EASY, ENGAGING GAMES FOR THREE OR MORE PLAYERS

Games requiring no equipment

Color Tag

One player is chosen as IT. All players except IT line up on one side of the yard. IT yells out a color. Every player wearing that color has to run across and reach the other side without being tagged.

Anyone tagged also becomes IT.

IT continues calling out different colors until all players have left the initial side of the yard.

All players who are now IT then turn around and face the remaining players, calling out one color at a time until everyone has crossed the yard or been tagged. This continues until the last player remains, who is now IT for the next game.

Shadow Tag

This popular twist on Tag can be played a couple of different ways. The basic idea is the same: one player is IT and chases the other players, tagging them by stepping on their shadows instead of tapping them with their hands.

With a smaller number of players, as few as two, whomever gets tagged can now be IT. However, with a large group, this could get confusing, since the players cannot feel that they have been tagged and may protest.

Instead, IT may call out the name of the player they tag, and that player may sit and count to ten before getting up and continuing to play.

After several minutes, it will be time to pause and choose a new IT for the next game.

Freeze Tag

There are two ways to play this classic. Of course, normal Tag rules apply: one player is IT, and runs around trying to tag everyone else.

Once someone is tagged, they must freeze in place. Other players can unfreeze by either 1) tagging the frozen player or 2) crawling through the legs of the frozen player.

The only rule with the latter is that IT cannot tag someone while they crawl! This continues for a set amount of time, and a new game begins with a new IT.

Blob Tag

One player is IT and stands in the center of the yard. The rest of the players line up along one side of the yard.

When IT says, "Go," the players run across to the other side and try not to get tagged. Anyone who is tagged joins IT in the center, and they must hold hands as they try to tag the runners.

As more people join the chain, the "blob" gets bigger and bigger and harder to escape. The last person not tagged is IT for the next game.

Octopus Tag

This game goes by many names, but the rules remain the same. Again, all players except one line up on one end of the yard, and the remaining player is IT and stands in the center.

On "Go," all the players try to cross the yard without being tagged. Once tagged, the players must freeze in their spot, but they can use their arms to try to tag other players as they run past – like octopi.

The last player standing is IT for the next round.

The game below is one of my absolute favorites and an excellent way to engage the fun-starved adults in your life.

Automatic Center Touch Football

This game is very inclusive – men or women of all ages can play it, with as few as three players and as many as 22, and any number in between. Any size football can be used. One person is chosen as the "full-time quarterback," who quarterbacks for both teams and calls the plays for them as well.

The game is usually played without kick-offs, and begins instead with a round of rock-paper-scissors. The winner is on offense first at the 20-yard line.

This game can be played on a short 40-yard field and first team on offense starts from the 20-yard line and can gain a first down with a 15-yard pick-up in four downs.

The quarterback huddles with the offense to call the play, then brings the offense to the line of scrimmage and has the ball in his/her hands for an automatic centering of the ball.

The game can be run out of any offensive formation and the defense has to count to 4-Missississppies before rushing the quarterback.

We usually played a two-hand touch game to make it harder than the usual one-handed touch for a tackle. The game was always fun and excellent for increasing passing, running, blocking and catching skills.

It also was a great aerobic exercise event, and if we played by a convenient water source we would take frequent water breaks and celebrate victories by jumping in the nearest sprinkler, pool, creek or lake.

Catch the Dragon's Tail

This game can be so much fun with a large group!

All players line up with their hands on the shoulders of the person ahead of them. The first player in line is the dragon's head; the last person is the tail.

The dragon's head leads the rest of the line – the dragon body – around in a chase to catch his tail. Everyone else has to hang on and keep up so that the line does not break apart.

Once the dragon's head catches the tail, the former tail becomes the new head and everyone else keeps the line in the same order. This way, everyone shifts down at the same rate, and each player gets a chance to play as both head and tail.

Hunter & Guard

This is a more complicated version of Tag.

In the center of the yard, you will need to set up a wide circle using some rope or rocks – it needs to be large enough to hold multiple players.

One player will be the guard, who will stay in the pen for the whole game. Another player will be the hunter, and the rest are the animals.

All of the animals run around the yard and try to avoid being tagged by the hunter. Once the hunter tags an animal, he leads them to the pen, where they remain until another animal comes and tags them to set them free.

Be careful, though – if the guard tags you while you try to free your friend, you will also be trapped in the pen!

The game can continue until every animal has been caught, or a smaller number of your choosing. Then you may begin a new game with a different hunter and guard.

Ants & Anteaters

If you have a large group that can work well together, this complex Tag game can be a huge hit!

The entire yard or a designated large section is now an anthill, and you will also need to choose a small "safe" area outside the anthill or in a corner of the yard.

All of the players are ants.

Depending on the size of your group, you may choose one or two players to be the anteaters, who chase the ants and try to tag them.

An ant that has been tagged must sit down and call out to the others for help. The ant can only be freed if two to four other ants gather around him, join hands and escort him as a group to the safe space.

The number of ants required to free one ant may change depending on the size and skill level of your entire group. Once the rescue has begun, all involved ants are off-limits until the rescue is complete. Stop the game every so often to switch anteaters so that everyone gets a chance to play!

Mother, May I?

This is yet another classic game.

One player stands at the far end of the yard, or closer if the players are younger. One at a time, the players call out, "Mother, may I take __ steps?" asking for a different number of steps each time.

The mother may answer "yes" or "no," and the player either moves or does not. The first person to reach the mother becomes the mother for the next round. Play may continue until everyone has had a chance to be the mother.

What Time is it, Mr. Fox?

This game is a fun twist on Mother, May I?

One player, the fox, stands at the far end of the space opposite the rest of the players, with his or her back to the others.

In unison, the players call out, "What time is it, Mr. Fox?" The fox then calls out a time, such as, "3 o'clock!" The players then take three steps towards the fox.

This means that the fox can have the players take as few as one step at a time, or as many as eleven. At one point, however, when the players ask the time, the fox cries, "Lunchtime!" and turns to chase the other players.

Older children will be clever enough to wait until the players are as close as possible, so that they will be easier to tag. The fox's goal is to tag one of the players, who plays the role of fox in the next round.

Follow the Leader

This classic game hardly requires an explanation.

One person is chosen to be the leader, and everyone forms a line behind him or her. The leader uses different movements to travel throughout the space, and the followers mimic them.

Leaders can walk, speedwalk, run, skip, jump, dance, walk in slow motion, march, walk backwards, hop on one foot, crawl ... the possibilities go on!

After some time, a new person gets to be the leader. This can continue until everyone has had a turn as the leader.

Simon Says

Again, this game is so well-known that the rules are obvious.

One player stands facing everyone else – this is "Simon." Simon tells the other players to do an action – touch your toes, do five jumping jacks, give your neighbor a high-five, etc.

But the players must only do that action if Simon begins their sentence with "Simon says."

Simon tries to trick the other players by occasionally by only saying the action: "Raise your hand!" instead of "Simon says, raise your hand."

If a player accidentally does the action, which Simon did not say to do, he or she is out until the next round. Simon's goal is to get everyone out.

The last player remaining is Simon for the next game.

Michelangelo's Madhouse

This is a cute twist on the classic "don't move or laugh!" game.

One player gets to be Michelangelo, who starts the game by spinning the other players one by one and letting them fall into a silly pose – they are now his statues.

Michelangelo then roams his museum trying to get his statues to laugh without touching them. Either the first statue to break or the last one standing becomes the next Michelangelo.

Helicopter (jump rope)

One player stands in front of the others, who form a half circle. This player holds one end of a jump rope in his or her hand and spins quickly in a circle while dragging the other end on the ground.

The players must jump over the rope before it touches them, or they are out. This is trickier than it sounds, so the game can go pretty quickly!

The last player standing holds the rope for the next round.

Ship to Shore

This is such a fun variation of Simon Says!

It can be played with groups of any size, so it would be perfect for an outdoor birthday party.

Instead of having the caller choose any silly movement, they have a few to choose from that center around a pirate ship theme.

It will only take a few minutes to teach all of the players what to do when the caller yells the appropriate words. Remember to switch callers every so often so that everyone has a turn.

When the caller cries:

"Port" – all players run to their left.

"Starboard" – all players run to their right.

"Bow" – all players run to the back of the yard.

"Hit the deck" – all players drop to the ground (safely!)

"Captain's coming" – everyone stands to attention, salutes, and says, "Aye, aye, captain."

"Man the lifeboats" – everyone has to grab hands with one partner; the last person left alone is out.

"Sharks" – everyone lies down on their backs with their limbs in the air.

Games played with a blindfold

Blind Man's Bluff

This is an old classic, best for groups of kids who already know each other. It will also be best played in a large, open space.

One child is selected to be the "blind man" first, and wears a blindfold. Everyone else spreads out, and the blind man wanders about trying to find the others.

Once the blind man touches someone, he or she has to guess who they have found. If they guess correctly, the person tagged becomes the new blind man; if not, play continues.

There is also a version of this game that is played like traditional tag: the blind man simply tries to tag someone, who becomes the blind man without having to be identified.

Either version would work well for a small group of players.

Find Your Friends

This game requires an adult chaperone and a few blindfolds.

Each player is to be blindfolded, and the adult spreads the players out from one another and spins them around a couple times before telling them "Go."

The players now have to find one another until they are all reunited.

The adult makes sure that no one wanders off or runs headfirst into each other.

If there are only two or three players, it can be made more challenging by allowing only one or two words to be spoken at a time – for example, "Here," or the player's own name – or by eliminating all talking.

Games played with a ball

Kick the Can

This is a slightly odd game, but simple enough for younger children to play.

You will need to set apart one section of the yard to be the "jail," and a can to kick. You may use a ball or similar object in place of an actual can.

One child is randomly selected to be IT. IT counts to 50 while the other players hide. Once everyone is hidden, IT wanders around searching for the others.

If IT spots someone, they say the person's name, and the race is on to kick the can.

If IT kicks the can first, the hider goes to jail. However, if the hider kicks the can before IT does, everyone in jail goes free. Then IT counts to 50 so that everyone can hide again.

Be sure to switch who is IT every few rounds.

Monkey in the Middle

This game can be played with any sort of light ball, from a beach ball for small children to a tennis ball for older players. A balloon would be very fun for younger players as well.

One player stands in between two others, who are spread out from one another. The outside players pass the ball back and forth over the "monkey's" head, trying to keep it out of his or her reach.

The monkey's goal is to intercept the ball. The player who last threw the ball becomes the new monkey in the middle.

As players progress in age and skill, they can stand further apart to increase the challenge of keeping the ball away from the player in the middle.

SPUD

This is an oldie but a goodie! SPUD is a great game for older kids because the rules are more complex than most catching games.

Each player is given a number, and the whole group stands in a circle around one player, who holds a ball. The player throws the ball straight up into the air and calls out a number.

The player with that number now has to catch the ball, preferably before it hits the ground. Everyone else scatters far away from the ball as soon as their numbers have not been called.

Once the chosen player has caught the ball, he or she yells, "SPUD!" and all the other players freeze. The player is allowed to take three large steps toward a frozen player, whom they try to tag by throwing the ball.

A frozen player may move their arms or torso to avoid getting hit, but their feet must stay planted on the ground.

If the ball hits a player, they receive the letter "S," and become the new person in the center. If the thrower misses the frozen player, he or she is still in the middle.

A player's second tag results in a "P," and so on until they spell "SPUD." Players who get all the way to SPUD are eliminated.

Steal the Bacon

This is a great game for a medium-sized group. One adult or older child can be the umpire.

You will need a random object to serve as the "bacon" – a ball, glove, Frisbee, etc.

Divide your group into two teams and assign each player a number; there should be an equal number of players on each team, so you should have two number ones, two twos, and so on.

The teams line up facing each other with the bacon in the center. The umpire calls out a random number, and both players with that number run to the bacon and try to grab it and carry it back to their team first without being tagged.

If a player succeeds, their team gets a point. If another runner tags the person who has the bacon, no points are awarded.

Play continues until a team gets 10 points. There will be multiple chances to try and steal the bacon.

Trigon

This game only requires three players, who form a triangle. There should be a good distance between the players.

One person starts out holding a ball. He or she uses their left hand to throw to the player on his or her right, who catches with their right hand.

That player then throws the ball to their right, also with their left hand, and so on.

Any player can switch the direction of play at any time to make the game more challenging. If a player drops the ball, whoever threw the ball gets one point.

Traditionally, the game ends when a player gets 21 points, but younger players can go to ten if they want a shorter game.

Most games and activities can be adapted to the skill and age of the players. The goal is to get the participants moving, laughing and having fun. For instance, here are some fun games to play with a group.

Snake in the Grass

This wonderful game can be played by people of all ages, and accommodates any number of participants.

It is held in a squared-off area and is best played on a mat-type surface (i.e., wrestling mats are great for this).

One person, "the snake," lies on his or her belly in the middle of the area. The other players are on their knees and can move anywhere so long as they stay within the boundaries of the designated area. The snake belly-crawls and tries to touch the scattering players.

If the snake touches someone, they are out of the game.

The game continues until one player is left and the snake either catches the player or gives up.

A twist to the game can be added where those touched by the snake also become a helping snake and team-up to touch the other players. This game promotes teamwork, stamina and strength building.

Here is another fun game I enjoyed as a kid. It is called 500. Have these games provoked memories of fun times you had as a child? What game could you teach your friends and family tonight?

500

Each spring, my friends and I looked forward to the baseball season, of which "500" was a high point.

One player was at bat, while the others were stationed in the outfield some 50 or so yards away. If someone caught the ball in the air they got 100 points; if the ball bounced once and then was caught, it was worth 75 points. Two bounces were worth 50 points, and a rolling grounder to stationary ball was worth 25.

If a player dropped the ball, they had to deduct the points the catch would have netted them; this was ample motivation for them player to excel. The first player that got to 500 points would get to bat and the batter would take the field to become an outfielder.

Throughout the game there was much trash talking amongst the players, a tool we used to get into each other's mind and hopefully create an advantage for ourselves.

This was one of the best parts of the game, adding fun and social dynamics no video game can provide.

Balloons (or Feathers) In the Air

The object of this activity is to keep the balloons, or feather up in the air and off the ground by blowing. Just pucker up and blow, and keep the balloons or feathers flying.

Games to Engage Adults

Listening Exercise

Objective: To demonstrate that most adults listen at about a 25% level of efficiency.

Procedure: Clip a story from a newspaper or magazine that is approximately two or three paragraphs long. With absolutely no introduction, casually mention to your group,... "Some of you probably saw the item in the paper the other day" and read aloud the entire article. When finished, you'll see a room of either bored or disinterested face. Pull out a dollar bill and state, "OK, I've got a few questions for you based and the story you just heard, and whoever gets them all right wins the dollar bill." Read eight to ten questions you have prepared (i.e., names, dates, places, etc.). In all likelihood, not one person will be able to answer all the questions correctly.

Discussion:

- You all heard the story, yet few could remember very much. Why (disinterest, no objective, no advance reward?)

- Why don't we listen? Is this typical? What can we do to sharpen our listening skills?

- If I had told you initially you could win some money, would you have listened more attentively? Why? How much would it take for you to listen carefully? How much do we hear when our clients or co-workers are talking?

Accentuate The Positive

Objective: To break down self-imposed barriers that don't allow people to "like themselves" and to enhance one's self image by sharing comments and personal qualities.

Procedure: Most of us have been brought up to believe that it is not "right" to say nice things about one's self or, for that matter, about others. This exercise attempts to change that attitude by having teams of two persons each share some personal qualities with one another.

In this exercise, each person provides his or her partner with the response to the following suggestions.

- Two **physical** attributes I like in myself
- Two **personality** qualities I like in myself
- One **talent** or **skill** I like in myself

Explain that each comment must be a positive one. No negative comments are allowed. Since most people will not have experienced such a positive encounter, it may take some gently nudging on your part to get them started.

Discussion Questions:

1. How many of you, on hearing the assignment, smiled slightly looked at your partner, and said, "You go first"?
2. Was this a difficult assignment for you?
3. How do you feel about it now?

Garage Sale

Objective: To help the participants to get to know each other.

Procedure: A table with a selection of goods that may be seen at a garage sale or junk drawer. The number of items needs to be more than the number of participants. A large sheet of paper or cloth is needed to cover the items from view until you are ready to begin.

1. Tell the participants to come up and select an item that for some reason resonates with them.

2. After everyone has selected an item, they are to introduce themselves to the group and state why that particular item appealed to them.

3. After everyone has introduced themselves ask the group if they thought the item selected by another participant helped them to get to know each other easier.

Everybody Wins-The Value of Cooperation

This training exercise shows how people look at the same task in different ways. Draw an imaginary line on the floor and ask one person to stand on each side.

Ask them to try to persuade the other to cross the line. After they try several ways, help them to discover that an easy way is to simply say, "If you'll cross the line, I will, too." Then they both win.

Use this activity and game to demonstrate the value of communication and cooperation.

Toilet Paper Game

Objective: To help the participants find connection with other members of the group.

Procedure: Pass around a roll of toilet paper and instruct the participants to "take how much you usually need."

It works best for each participant to take at least four or five squares. If someone takes fewer, add, "No one uses just two squares!"

For each square, the person is to tell the group one interesting fact about himself.

Getting Acquainted

Objective: To allow participants to become acquainted through a structured exercise.

Procedure: At the opening session of a group meeting, each individual is given a blank nametag. Each person completes the following items:

1. My name is _____

2. I have a question about_____

3. I can answer a question about_____

After being given a few minutes to respond to the statements, allow 10-15 minutes in which the group is encouraged to meet and mix with as many people as possible.

Online sources:
https://www.activityvillage.co.uk/outdoor-games
https://www.familyfuntwincities.com/outdoor-games-for-kids/
http://www.kidactivities.net/outdoor-games-for-school-age-kids/#top
http://www.greatgroupgames.com/steal-the-bacon.htm
http://www.group-games.com/action-games/spud-game.html
http://myplaygroundgames.blogspot.com/2010/03/captains-coming.html

100 Training Games – Gary Kroehnert
Games Trainers Play – Edward E. Scannell

ABOUT THE AUTHOR

Bob Hermes wants to dedicate this book to his three grandchildren, Madeline, Cooper and Evie Mae and hope they will all enjoy playing with their friends and family. Their parents learned that play is free, joyful and multi-generational, and hopefully they will too.

Bob Hermes, was born in Williston, North Dakota, in 1957 and moved with his family to Missoula, Montana, in 1963.

The family loved and participated in every sport and everything done outdoors — fishing, hiking, camping, skiing, biking – you name it. Sports and play were a major part of everyday life.

Bob was educated in Missoula public schools, graduating from Missoula Sentinel High School in 1975, The University of Montana in 1980 (B.A., R-TV), Gonzaga 2013 (M.A., Comm-Leadership).

He is married to Linda, his lovely wife of 39 years, (at the time of this book's publishing) and has two grown athletic boys, Jason and John, who were excellent athletes and enjoyed sports and playing for the sake of fun. Both Jason and John are wonderful fathers now, and keep fun a focus in their children's lives.

Bob coached youth football and wrestling for more than 30 years, and officiated football, wrestling and volleyball for three decades as well.

He has experienced the best life lessons of sports and play. He has also seen some of the ugly sides of overbearing parents who pushed children too hard to win at all costs, shutting down their willingness to try and continue to succeed for fear of letting down others.

Bob is indebted to his family, friends and mentors who have helped him along the way to learn the best of life lessons from play.

They have set the example of just playing for fun and connection.

He would especially like to thank his University of Montana Physical Education Professor, George Cross. It was from him that Bob gained excellent mentoring in the instruction of how to administer games for teachers and other adults.

Professor Cross taught for decades at University of Montana and passed along his wisdom to hundreds if not thousands of physical education teachers over the years. George was a special person and Bob owes him a heart-felt thanks along with his legendary wrestling coach Jug Beck of Sentinel High School.

Both Jug and George understood the value of mixing hard work and fun in life.

BOB HERMES

AFTERWORD

Brian Cooper

After reading Bob's book, my first thought was if just one parent takes the time to turn off the TV, put the cell phone down and actually spend time playing with their child it's a homerun!

That being said, my true hope is that millions of parents, coaches, and educators across the country take the time to read *Go Play!*

Talk about bringing back the greatest childhood memories of good ole fashion play. My mind immediately went back to chasing my father around the house with a tennis ball playing Red Rover and once we tired him out progressing to "Kick the Can" with the neighborhood gang.

Bob takes us through an emotional journey on the lost art of play and its sobering impact on today's society. *Go Play!* shows a true labor of love filled with interesting facts, fastidious research and heart wrenching stories.

A great twist throughout the book is that you will find an array of games and how they are played.

I have been involved in coaching youth sports most of my life and this book will be a requirement for my parents from now on.

Well done Bob!

Printed in Great Britain
by Amazon